THE BRAVE

a collection of poetry and prose

edited by Rachael Ikins & Heidi Nightengale

The Brave $15.99

Edited by Rachael Ikins & Heidi Nightengale
Cover design by Laura Williams French
Clare Songbirds Publishing House Poetry Series
ISBN 978-1-947653-79-5
Clare Songbirds Publishing House
The Brave © 2019 Clare Songbirds Publishing

Printed in the United States of America
FIRST EDITION

Clare Songbirds Publishing House Mission Statement:
Clare Songbirds Publishing House was established to provide
a print forum for the creation of limited edition, fine art from
poets and writers, both established and emerging. We strive to
reignite and continue a tradition of quality, accessible literary
arts to the national and international community of writers, and
readers. Chapbook manuscripts are carefully chosen for their
ability to propel the expansion of art and ideas in literary form.
We provide an accessible way to promote the art of words in
order to resonate with, and impact, readers not yet familiar with
the siren song of poets and writers. Clare Songbirds Publishing
House espouses a singular cultural development where poetry
creates community and becomes commonplace in public places.

140 Cottage Street
Auburn, New York 13021
www.claresongbirdspub.com

Contents

Introduction

This book was compiled after Laura Williams French, owner/publisher of Clare Songbirds, saw the episode of Returning the Favor featuring Semper K9. Semper K9's mission to help veterans inspired her to reach out with an idea for a book about military life written by veterans and their families. All royalties from this book will be donated to Semper K9.

Semper K9's mission is unlike any other. Semper K9 not only utilizes rescue dogs in their service dog selection process, they also custom train each dog to the specific needs of their wounded veterans. They provide training and support for the entire family. Through the Family Integration Program, they teach caregivers and other family members the skills needed to support the veteran in their recovery through animal-assisted therapy. Using rescued and donated dogs, they provide mental health mobility service dogs free of charge to wounded service members to enhance their quality of life.

This book was curated by Clare Songbirds editor Rachael Ikins and owner/editor Heidi Nightengale. Rachael reached out to numerous writer's groups encouraging veterans and their families to submit. Everyone involved in this project has been deeply touched by the stories and poems that the authors have shared. We are proud to give a voice to so many veterans and their families.

About Semper K9

Combat veteran founded and operated, Semper K9's mission is to enhance the quality of life for wounded, critically ill and injured members of the U.S. Armed Forces and their families by providing them assistance dogs. Using rescued and donated dogs they provide service dogs for psychiatric alert and mobility challenges free of charge to wounded service members.

According to the Veterans Administration, 834,463 veterans from OIF/OEF suffer from combat-related PTSD–that is 30%. Overall there are 10.6 million veterans living with combat-related PTSD.

Every 11 seconds, an animal is euthanized in the US. Semper K9 is helping make a difference in those figures by rescuing dogs from the shelter and training them to be service dogs for wounded service members at no cost. By enhancing the quality of life for service members and their families Semper K9 is able to help them regain confidence and independence.

What began in 9th grade joining the MCJROTC program became the beginning of a long road to the right path. USMC combat veteran Christopher Baity is still on that path heading toward success after service. Joining the Marine Corps right after high school, Baity wanted to be a military working dog handler.

"We came to DC for a JROTC field trip. While in the area we visited the kennels at Marine Corps Base Quantico. I was the first one to volunteer to 'catch a dog.' After that experience I knew I wanted to become a Military Working Dog Handler," said Baity. After graduating boot camp at MCRD Parris Island, Baity went to Marine Combat Training (MCT) at Camp Lejeune and then on to Military Police (MP) School in Ft Leonard Wood, MO. At the time he enlisted, the path to becoming a Marine Corps MWD Handler was to first become an MP. Upon graduation from MP school, Baity was selected to attend MWD Handler's Course at Lackland Air Force Base with the 341st Training Squadron. Afterward, Baity was given the opportunity to create a kennel program at then HQ Marine Corps Henderson Hall, and he took it. He was stationed there throughout most of his military career, becoming the kennel master in 2005 after his first deployment to Iraq.

Being named 'Top Dog' at MWD Handler school put Baity at the top of the list to join a selected few Marines to attend a 'Train the Trainer" course with the Israeli Defense Force (IDF) Oketz Dog School. "I was honored to be selected by the Marine Corps MWD Program Manager to attend SSD school is Israel," said Baity. "The experience was invaluable toward my future endeavors to become an advanced dog trainer." This experience also gave him a skill that not many dog trainers have, the ability to teach others how to train dogs.

Upon completion of this nine-month program, Baity had two billets in the Marine Corps. When he was stateside he was an SSD Section Trainer when he was deployed; he was Regional Kennel Master and SSD Team Leader. His next two deployments in the Marine Corps were to Iraq, attached to the 5th Engineer Battalion with the United States Army, in and around Baghdad. After his active duty service, Baity deployed to Afghanistan as a Contract Explosive Detector Dog Handler with RONCO Corporation as part of Afghanistan Central Command.

When he returned home from deployments, Baity faced bouts of post-traumatic stress disorder (PTSD) as well as drug and alcohol use. Like many service members coming home from combat and trying to transition back into family life, it can be a difficult shift. "Trying to find purpose after the transition to civilian life is difficult," he said. "Lack of job security, tumultuous family dynamic and the desire to continue serving weighs heavily on your mind every day." For several years Baity felt at a loss, going from one contracting job to another.

Semper K9 rescues dogs from shelters and trains them to be service dogs at no cost for disabled service members. "I wanted to take my skills the Marine Corps taught me and my post-deployment challenges to assist other veterans to overcome their own difficulties," Baity said. He and his wife, Amanda, founded Semper K9 in 2014 and went right to work. After researching other organizations that had similar missions, they identified weakness in other groups and strengths from industry leaders to create what currently has a one hundred percent success rate with their services.

"The most important things to us were to utilize rescue dogs and ensure that our veterans are assisted at no cost to them," said Baity. "Also, being a military family with small children, the family involvement was high on our list of priorities since our mission is to enhance the quality of life for our wounded veterans." Because of his dedication to Semper K9's mission, Baity was awarded American Heroes Channel's Red Bandanna Hero in 2016 and named a Washingtonian of the Year for 2017 by *Washingtonian* magazine and in 2019 he was honored by Washington Business Journal as a veteran servant leader in the Metro DC area.

Baity's success after service now radiates down to his five children; the oldest has eyes on Marine Corps OCS. "I am beyond thankful to have the support of a loving wife and children along with our team of volunteers." Semper K9 currently boasts 125 plus volunteers for a relatively small organization. "I feel like the many trials I endured during combat deployments, and the transition afterward have paved the way for my continued life of service," said Baity.

For all those who serve
and their families

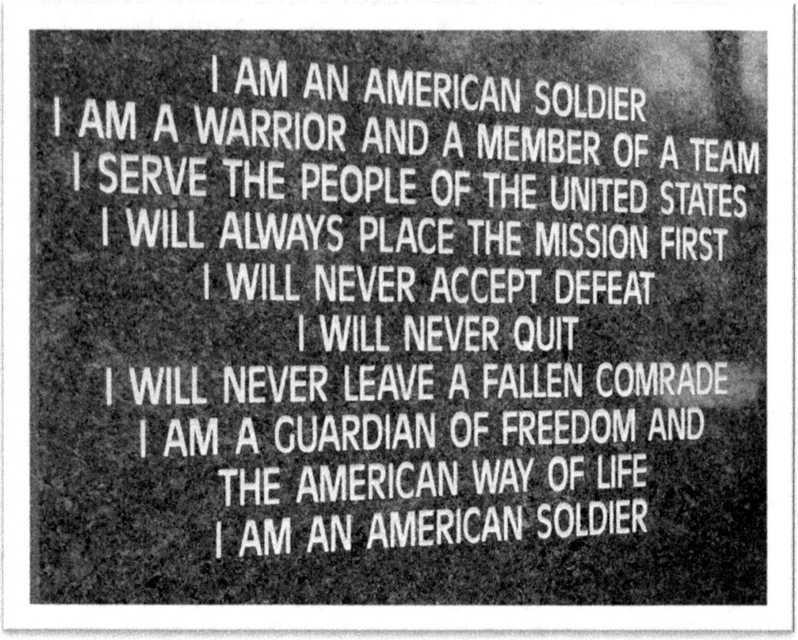

I AM AN AMERICAN SOLDIER
I AM A WARRIOR AND A MEMBER OF A TEAM
I SERVE THE PEOPLE OF THE UNITED STATES
I WILL ALWAYS PLACE THE MISSION FIRST
I WILL NEVER ACCEPT DEFEAT
I WILL NEVER QUIT
I WILL NEVER LEAVE A FALLEN COMRADE
I AM A GUARDIAN OF FREEDOM AND
THE AMERICAN WAY OF LIFE
I AM AN AMERICAN SOLDIER

THE SOLDIER

The Grunt
Mike Kanner

How long 'til rest will come
When will the mission end.
Patrol is long and hard
My country I defend

I've borne this ruck of sorrow
And drank canteens of tears
All hoping for mission's end
Along the many years.

I've humped and pulled
And bowed my back in pain
I've plodded long and hard
And yet here I remain

A thousand miles from nowhere
Along with just my fears
If I die, so far away
Will someone shed some tears?

Someday, someone will lift it off
Someday, someone will take it away
Until that time, I march on
Until my dying day.

There Is a History in His Feet
Sandra Flores-Surprise

There is a history in his feet.

His swollen, bloody, mangled feet casually wrapped
in useless gauze and tattered bandages
that divulge crimson-colored blotches of blood and pink seepage.

I believe not for the first time.

I imagine him a young man.
Exuberant in his youth, still bright-eyed to the world…

green to the Army.

I see him, in my mind's eye, imbedded in the brutal, unforgiving
jungles of Vietnam;
his feet bloody through the tattered bandages and
perpetually soaked Army boots;
the only pair he was issued.

How many miles and miles and miles he must have marched
through dense vegetation,
over treacherous terrain,
always, *always* in the rain.

Through harrowing fields of landmines,
over flooded streams,
 in perpetually soaked socks and weatherworn leather boots
now molded to his tortured feet.

Oh, the distance his feet have travelled.
Oh, the hell they have walked him through and back.

Now they carry him through the veterans' hospital entrance.

There is a history in his feet.

Medal Winner
William Conelly

Accept him afterwards,
wedged upright on a sofa,
tunneling the sunset:
nights aren't night enough.
Why this is so you will
not fully understand;

he can't explain himself:
Look how hot, bleeding
turmoil's been transfused
by cooler, kinder stuff
and weeping men still
emerge to grip my hand.

You're Painting WHAT?

Joan Applebaum

Well, they always say you never know where inspiration might strike and I guess this proves that "they", (whoever they are) are right.

Whenever I am painting a still life, I usually look for interesting objects to group together or objects that somehow tell a story. But every once in a while, a mundane object, something I don't usually consider as an item to paint will beckon me. In this case it was the combat boots. My son Ben had left them behind, when he was home on leave in summer 2011.

The boots were probably left behind intentionally because they didn't fit well. Ask any military person about their boots and you are likely to get a long story about the trials and tribulations of finding just the right boot. The right boot is usually never the one they were issued; nearly always the one they had to pay for later. But...I digress. Somehow I kept looking at those boots, deciding; acrylic? watercolor? pencil? And why? Why do I want to paint the boots? They really hadn't gotten to the point of being beaten down and grubby...artists always love that stuff. But they did appeal to me.

Maybe because it would force my left brain to pay attention to a right brained activity as I made sure I painted every turn of the laces as they wove in and out of the eyelets. Hmmm. Maybe... But most likely I was intrigued by the universal symbolism of the combat boot. The boots, more than any other part of the uniform, show the wear and tear of the daily routine of the soldier. I had read an article written by a soldier's wife who lived in military housing. She mentioned the eerie stillness of the housing development when the troops were deployed. When they are gone one of the things you miss is the sound of their boots on the stairs in the early morning hours as they leave for work.

So with all of those thoughts circling around in my mind, I painted the boots in watercolor. My left brain was intrigued by the laces and the eyelets and my right brain was just happy to paint. My heart was feeling the loneliness of the sound of no boots on the stairs.

I later used the painting in a graphic design incorporating the traditional Irish verse below.

May the road rise up to greet you, may all your days be bright,
May love walk by your side by day and keep you warm by night,
May all you meet along the way be glad to call you friend
And may the road rise up to greet you, and bring you home again.

For all of those young men and women scattered across the world serving their country - may the road rise up to greet you and bring you home again.

©2019 Joan Applebaum

These Colors We Die For...
Emmanuel Kane

The bugle blasts.
We start to march again, left, right, left, right.
Our bodies loaded with bullet bags, heads burning with fire, we
sing war songs.

With our guns asleep on our shoulders
our faces vile, we march swinging our right arm, left, right, left,
right.

We march through twilight,
our boots smash gravel and sand.

We march towards glory and death.
Young and foolish, joyful and hopeful, we march on,
shelling hours.

Undisclosed Location
Dario R. Beniquez

When I went over there, we were at war.
The weather was wet and cold, temperature 30 degrees.

In Frankfurt, security agents said, "Take photos of everything.
Exercise caution. Your body is a loudspeaker."

Deployed, I was in an army tent with three fellows.
The language symbols masked with noise. The runway
unpaved, broken airfield lights populated its end.

Ahmad, the engineer, saw this.
His mind calculated the ratio of runway strip to target zone.

Ramón, an architect, an artist, painted, on a steno pad,
the landscape, storage sheds, an air control tower in repairs,
troops in winter's shadow.

I translated the unreal to the real—lines on a map to roadways,
water towers, buildings, gunnery range, ammo igloos, bunkers.

Roger, a naval intelligence officer, the surveillance leader,
memorized vehicle movements, consolidated photos
and notes—reported to headquarters.

Back in Frankfurt, we briefed the colonels. Back in the States,
my mind settles nowhere

Bennett's Tonsorial Emporium
Ronald Milburn

"Bennett needs a shoe-shine boy," my father announced.

"Wow, a job!"

"You'd work for tips. Are you interested?"

"You bet."

"Good. Bennett said you could start on Saturday."

My father took my brothers and me to Bennett's for haircuts since before I could remember. When I was very young and too short to sit in the chair, Bennett placed a board across the arms and removed my locks as I squirmed.

It had been my older brother's job for five summers, but he'd recently enlisted in the Marine Corp. It was the summer of 1967, and I'd recently celebrated my thirteenth birthday. My mother cried as I enjoyed birthday cake because her oldest boy was departing the next day for boot camp. Another brother was in the Navy off the coast of Vietnam. The following day, our family waived at the Ft. Pendleton bound man's ascending plane as I excitedly anticipated my first day at my new job.

For thirty years the candy-cane barber pole turned continuously outside Bennett's Tonsorial Emporium. Through the glass-front, one could see customers in brown leather chairs with chrome handles enjoying their wait. It was jokingly called the 'liar's section.' A plaque on the wall proclaimed, Only Two Lies And One Fib Per Customer, Please. A bell above the door regularly jingled to announce the arrivals and departures.

Few men entered anticipating or desiring rapid service. By-passing the conversation would be akin to gulping Champagne rather than sipping languidly. In fact, the infrequent mother with a shaggy-haired boy in tow was allowed without complaint to the front of the line. Had he arrived with his father he would have steeped a while in the tobacco smoke to witness the testosterone-laden ritual.

The owner of the establishment was Bennett Rardin, but everyone called him by his first name. He was the son of Irish immigrants named O'Rardin who 'Americanized' the name at Ellis Island. He was small in stature but large in presence. He compensated for his height with broad hand gestures and a booming voice. His positive and friendly disposition was enormously contagious.

He'd often invite a customer to his chair with a low bow. Then, exaggerating his Irish accent, he'd say, "Come ye vagabond and sit on the throne whilst I relieve you of your heavy burden."

Once seated he'd waive the smock flamboyantly like a Spanish Matador aggravating a bull before allowing the satin to settle on his entertained patron. He made everyone feel special. As if they were the reason, he opened his shop that day.

Bennett seldom asked a customer for instruction because he was familiar with nearly every scalp. Some came in for a shave, so he'd recline the chair and apply a hot towel over their beard. While the whiskers stiffened, Bennett, with great flair, would sharpen the straight razor on a leather strap which dangled from the side of the red leather chair. He'd dance for our amusement to the rhythm of the blade slapping the cowhide. Once the skin was lobster red and the stubble was standing at attention, he'd apply the shaving cream. Years of experience allowed Bennett to rapidly foam a face with a soft bristle brush without splashing soap in an eye. Then, with long smooth strokes, his skilled hand would efficiently remove the lather to reveal smooth skin. A stinging splash of after-shave awakened the reclining client and announced his completion.

As the patron exited, if I had no customer, I'd drop from my stool located across from Bennett and sweep the floor. This would allow my boss a few seconds to draw on his ever-smoldering cigarette. In appreciation, he'd sometimes buy my lunch.

As the barbers worked, everyone watched, talked, and laughed. I loved listening to the stories. The men discussed sports, complained about their jobs, or debated politics. The most common conversation that summer was the war in Vietnam.

Someone who served in Europe in World War II said, "If Ike were in charge we'd already be done in Vietnam."

Another man, who'd served in the Pacific, retorted "We need a good general like MacArthur. He knew how to chase the enemy out of the palm trees."

World War II ended more than 20 years prior, but memories were fresh and opinions firm. Almost every customer had served overseas during World War II or a few years later in Korea. Bennett had served in North Africa.

The other barber was as tall as Bennett was short. Everyone just called him "Stretch." He fought in the Philippines in ferocious battles with hand-to-hand combat. Stretch harbored bitter feelings, and he didn't mind vocalizing his opinions.

"We fought them in the jungles and beat them," he proclaimed, holding his comb in one hand and scissors in the other. "Only one way to deal with the Viet Cong," he added, holding the scissors against his client's neck.

One man, about my father's age, climbed onto my shoe-shine chair. His name was Mr. Lannon. He wore brown cowboy boots and asked me to shine them almost every Saturday.

Every week he'd say, "Son, use black polish and eventually they'll turn black."

I rolled up his pant legs and started applying the shoe cream. Though I polished and buffed them every week, they never turned black.

Mr. Lannon fought the German's in France where he left a lung. He claimed he saw the smoke burst from the rifle that shot him. The bullet traveled through his jacket, entered his abdomen, and bounced off some bones. At the time he was injured he had gloves inside his jacket which the hot bullet ignited. The burning gloves cauterized the wound and probably saved his life.

During World War II he was stationed in England waiting for the Allied forces to invade France to free the French people from Hitler's army. A few days after the D-day invasion he was sent across the English Channel as a reinforcement.
"Hedgerows," he blurted, as I tried to polish his moving boots.

"Those blasted hedgerows," he continued. "The Germans hid behind them and picked us off like ducks on a pond."
In his excitement, he kicked forward causing me to smear black polish on his pants.

"They knew we were coming down those paths, so they ambushed us," he said, pointing to the scar hidden beneath his blue work shirt. "It's no different in 'Nam," he bellowed.
 Both barbers stopped clipping hair to listen.

"You've just got to keep pushing," he said, nearly shouting as he placed his boot back on my stand. "You can't stop and hold your ground."

"That's how General Patton did it," he hollered, raising his arm in the air.

"Old Blood and Guts said, 'When you're scared, you've just got to keep pushing forward' and that's what we did, too. We chased them all the way back to Berlin."

In his excitement, his cigarette ashes fell on my hair. His boots were a moving target.

Completing his story, he leaned back, looked down, and said, "You going to take all day, boy."

When I finished, I hoped he wouldn't notice the polish on his pants.

The bell above the door clanged. Everyone turned at once to see Toby pushed in a wheelchair by his girlfriend.

Toby could feel the staring eyes. To ease the tension he shouted, "Hi, everybody."

Everyone responded almost in unison, "Hi, Toby." "Almost done," Stretch exclaimed as he brushed the hair from his customer's neck. "I'll be right with you."

His customer stepped from the barber chair, paid, and left. Slim pointed to a spot and said, "You're next, Toby."

No one complained when he was moved to the head of the line. Stretch had been cutting Toby's hair since his return from Vietnam. Toby was a local hero. Still keeping his military hair-cut required weekly visits. Previously Toby sat in his wheelchair while Stretch snipped and clipped.

"Not this time!" Toby proclaimed as his girlfriend pushed his wheelchair forward. "I'll sit in the barber chair," he exclaimed with a smile. "I've got new legs, and I need to practice using them."

Bennett paused to watch Toby push himself up to a standing position. He took two steps then wrestled, stepped, and twisted until he was seated. Stretch pumped, and the chair ascended.

"Wonderful!" proclaimed Bennett.

"That's amazing," said Stretch. "How long have you had legs?"

"Just a few weeks," Toby responded. "I've practiced until my stubs are sore, but I'm anxious to get back on two feet," he replied as he smiled.

"Good for you," Stretch proclaimed as he put the cape around Toby.

"I know it's been hard to cut my hair in that wheelchair, especially since you're so tall. Thanks. A lot."

Stretch merely patted his friend on the shoulder then ran a comb through his short hair.

Bennett finished with his customer and proclaimed, "Next victim, please."

An old man rose slowly and walked forward with the aid of a cane. He wore a handsome suit with a fresh carnation in his lapel. As he approached he removed his hat and handed it to Bennett.

"How are you today, Doctor," Bennett asked as he placed the black cape over the silver-haired man's shoulders.

"I'm doing just fine, thank you.".

He wasn't really a doctor but, in the First World War, he had been a medic. The troops called him 'Doc' and it stuck. In the barbershop many men went by a nickname or rank, they earned in the war. Some men were called 'Sarge' which was short for sergeant. 'Chief' was a nickname of a chief petty officer and 'Gunny' had been a gunnery sergeant. If someone had achieved the rank of colonel, they were respectfully called 'Colonel' the rest of their lives.

Doc owned the funeral home in our town. He was usually quiet, but today he voluntarily spoke. "I got some heartbreaking news today, Bennett."

Doc had buried a relative for everyone there, so he was accustomed to sad news, but "heartbreaking news" made all heads turn.

"I got a call today from the army." He paused then continued, "Billy Branch got killed in Vietnam. They're shipping his body home."

No one said anything, trying to absorb the news. Some shook their heads in disbelief. Billy was the first Vietnam fatality from our town, and everyone knew him. He'd been a basketball star in high school and held several school records.

Bennett dropped his hands to his side, shook his head, and said, "Tell me it isn't so. He's such a nice boy and from such a nice family." He continued, "I've known him forever. I gave him his first haircut on his first birthday. His father took pictures while his mother entertained him so he wouldn't cry."

"The Marines are sending an escort with his body," Doc said.

"That's good," Stretch commented.

Bennett started cutting Doc's hair again.

"How?", someone asked.

"Don't know for sure," Doc replied. "I just know we can have an open casket.

"Well, that's a good thing. I mean, for his mother's sake," Bennett added.

"Yes, somehow it helps a mother's grief to see her son and say goodbye."

One man wearing a VFW hat asked, "Does the family want a military service?"

"Of course."

"I'll tell the men at the VFW, so they can prepare," the veteran responded as he lit a cigarette.

He inhaled deeply then exhaled the smoke which added to the haze.

"We'll give him a fine send off. He'll have an honor guard. We won't be short of volunteers, that's for sure. Most everyone at the VFW and the American Legion will be there."

Toby spoke for the first time since Doc's revelation and muttered, "Freedom isn't free."

Stretch added, "I hope we win this war and come home soon."

"I hope he didn't suffer," someone mumbled.

For a long time, the only sound heard was scissors. Most just looked at the floor or stared out the large glass window. Maybe some remembered Billy in good times. Possibly others stared into decades-old battlefields, wondering why men like Billy died, but they came home.

Bennett changed the subject.

"How's that foot today, Doc?"

"A bit worse than usual. I think we're in for a change in the weather. Those missing toes are throbbing."

"Missing toes?" Bennett asked. "I don't remember how you lost those toes. Better tell me again,"

He'd heard the story many times, but he just wanted someone to fill the painful silence.

"I lost them in the Big War. You know, World War One," Doc said, projecting his voice for the audience of willing spectators. "I spent 1917 and 1918 in a cold, wet trench in

France. The German's were dug-in fifty yards from us. We could see them, and they saw us. I spent months in those trenches shooting and being shot at."

I'd never heard the story, and Doc directed his attention toward me as I listened intently from atop my perch on my shoe-shine stool.

"One winter morning in early 1918 word came down the line, we were going to attack. On signal, we crawled out and charged. Being a medic, I carried a satchel of medical supplies instead of a rifle. I hadn't run ten yards when the first man fell. I wrapped gauze around his head. It stopped the bleeding, and an aide carried him back to our line. The fighting was brutal but only lasted a short while. The assault was a failure, as usual. Our troops retreated, but I stayed to treat the wounded."

Bennett turned Doc toward the mirror for approval, then spun him back to face me.

"Normally the enemy didn't shoot our medics, and we avoided shooting theirs. I was carrying a wounded soldier when a bullet ripped into my leg. Before I could fall, another went through my shoulder and into the soldier I was carrying."
Doc continued, "I fell into a shallow ditch and tried not to scream. Once I got over the initial shock, I reached into my bag for morphine. After an injection, I felt some relief and pushed a bandage into my shoulder then wrapped my bleeding leg.

" I checked my patient who was unconscious. Nothing I could do for him except plug his wounds.

There was silence except for Doc and an occasional match striking as someone lit their cigarette.

"I didn't try to move to safety for fear some German would finish me off," he continued.

"How long did you lie there," I blurted out.

"All day and all night, and the next day, too," Doc answered. "It was fiercely cold on that battlefield. I nestled against my patient so we could share body heat. We were face to face on that frozen ground. He was a young private with dark hair and brown eyes. As he exhaled his breath fogged in the cold air. The second day his breathing became shallow. He died before the sunset day."

Doc looked at the ceiling and recollected, "A few hours later, we got bad weather, and the clouds covered the moon. It was very dark, and I figured it was safe to move. I gave myself more morphine in preparation for my escape. Slowly and quietly I pulled myself from that ditch across the snow and mud. I pulled with my good arm and pushed with my good leg. The pain was excruciating. I was weak, but somehow made it to our line and someone pulled me to safety. I don't remember being carried to a field hospital, but by the time we arrived, I was semiconscious. The toes on my injured leg were black from frostbite and low circulation. The orderly removed my boot, and three fell off, but I didn't feel it."

Bennett brushed the hair from Doc's neck and removed the cape. Doc leaned forward toward me with a penetrating stare.

"I left those toes in France, young man, but I still feel them. The pain is a constant reminder of my patient whose warmth kept me alive. When bad weather approaches, like it did in France, I can feel them throb. In my dreams, I feel the phantom toes and see the dead soldier's face. I think I always will."

Bennett handed Doc his hat. Silence followed the undertaker, who limped toward the door. He removed his suit jacket from a hook, but before buttoning it, he removed a cigar from the inside pocket. Once lit he reached for the doorknob. As he opened the door, he turned back and tipped his hat.

Scanning his audience, he said, "Won't be frostbite in Vietnam. But it'll be hell."

The bell above the door clanged as he left. Stretch finished Toby's haircut then everyone watched as he maneuvered to his wheelchair. His girlfriend pushed him to the door as some-one held it open.

Still, no one was talking. Finally, Bennett jumped in the air and clicked his heels like a leprechaun.

"Who amongst you with ten toes would like a haircut?"

His next victim jumped from his seat and hurried forward.

Bennett, wishing to lighten the mood, said, "So, are you a Cubs fan or Cardinals?"

As he placed the apron around his patron's neck, I slumped on my stool and pondered the gravity of what I'd heard.
Billy was dead and wouldn't come home with exciting stories.

Some like Doc, Toby, and Mr. Lannon, wore permanent physical scars from injuries acquired in hellish battles.
Unfortunately, Toby's battles never ended. His scars were more

severe than his missing legs. He struggled for a few years before he ended his own life.

Each day that summer, I listened to veterans recount their experiences that seemed so fantastic, but that morning they seemed less glorious. While sitting atop a shoe-shine chair in a smoke-filled barbershop, I thought of my two older brothers. For the first time, I was afraid for them.

On Veteran's Day
Peggy Seely

Fritz immigrated to America at the age of ten
Lied about his age to join the US Navy
to fight against his homeland in WWI
When his father died soon after, he was released

on a hardship discharge, never went to sea.
Bernard joined the US Army to fight in WWII
Spent weeks in the base hospital
fighting pneumonia, never saw a battlefield.

Joe joined the Coast Guard, spent his days
patrolling the coastline, throwing meatballs at seagulls
for entertainment; his mother saved ration stamps
to buy a half-pound of hamburger to feed her kids at home.

Tom joined the US Navy to fight in Korea, his ship
an Experimental Destroyer Escort, New London, CT
testing submarine-seeking sonar; sailed away
to Bermuda; on hot days he swam in the pool at the Club.

Jerry had the next draft number of all the boys in town
called to fight in Vietnam but the war stopped
before he got in it; he was willing and ready, though.
All of the above were Ready. Willing. Able.

No battle scars, no PTSD, no stories of sacrifice and valor.
No buddy ever died in their arms. They didn't starve or freeze.
To each of them, do I say "Thank you for your service?"
You bet your sweet ass I do!

Army Veteran
Dario R. Beniquez

I ask my daughter
do you want to look through the window.

She nods. We both look,
our heads pressed against a tiny porthole.

Inside, we see a bare concrete room.

On top of a conveyor belt sits a cardboard box.

I can only see one end.

I see my brother.

He wears a white gown that covers his shaved head.

He looks like a saint.

I see the side of his face,
his still black beard.

He is extremely serious.

I remember that look that expression, the one he
would give me when I borrowed his jacket

without asking.

My daughter's face turns as the conveyor moves into
the blue-white flames.

Short Story
Arthur Ramer

I'm reading a book of short stories
written thirty thousand years ago
in nineteen eighty-nine.

If there are veterans
they're dressed in jeans, wear beards
and long hair. Swig whiskey
from tall glasses and refer obliquely to
the 'Nam.

I close the book on my chest
and marvel at how many more
vets there are now.
All in the name of God
and country and family,
baseball and booze.

Time has slipped away,
wetting swamps and sands.
I'm amazed at how we've wasted away
the fortune of our future
into futility.

Uniform
Fee Thomas

We put them on our children,
our young eighteen year olds
We have them stitched up so nice,
tidy and clean
The thread laying in perfect rows of straight lines
Obeying just like the wearer will
The lines of the garment straight
prepared, alert
The angles fixed, steady
always ready for what may be coming
Color varying depending on environment and need
We put these uniforms on our children
and usher them to war
The children do not know that that same uniform
is an extreme form of camouflage
once they are Veterans
Once home from war, they will no longer be seen.
We put them on our children,
our young eighteen year olds
We have them stitched up so nice
tidy and clean
The thread laying in perfect rows of straight lines
Obeying just like the wearer will

Reservist Lament
Tony Daly

Holding you in my arms,
Stretching from chin to knee,
Your "nook" grew smaller.
Where has time gone?
To work, to overtime, to
Lands where bullets chirp
More prevalently than birds.

And when I'm home, I'm not really home.
40 hours of necessary monotony,
Plus mandatory overtime.
One weekend a month was only
One weekend before you drew breath.
The year I spent away
Was a fourth of your life since.

Now I'm home. Do you know me?
Your father, daddy, dada.
The hug I knew has changed.
The arms and legs are longer,
But don't squeeze as tight.
The yearning to keep separation
At bay is no longer as persistent.
I fear that will not return,
Cause I'm home, but not really here.

As I hold you, my mind slips,
To unpleasantness I hope you never see,
To losses I suffered so you wouldn't.
Perhaps your love isn't less with age,
But more distant with my mind.
Can we ever get that back?
When I deploy again, will it come back?
And the next time, will it come back?

MILITARY FAMILY

Family Photograph
Laurie Kolp

I am the after-military wife and these are my after-military kids
clad in khaki pants and starched white shirts, a picture-perfect life
of after-military bliss. We eat at the same table every night in the
same small house where outside hangs an American flag over red
roses all the same since I married my Marine after his stint in the
military. Since our family's beginning, shortly after his military
life and after the laughter returned, no transfers have uprooted us
or disturbed our sense of steadfastness. In fact, this family portrait
might make you think he never took a risk for his life: the drink
that nearly killed him.

Redeployed
Catherine Zickgraf

She crochets upstairs
from his lonely chair,
tuning out the rockets of July-smoke sky.

For bills not flags, yet
she chained her youth
to the steel of his military-morgue toe-tag.

Under lashes like willows, still she weeps,
feeling how his fingers
last brushed along hers.

Her dreams pull skeins,
and months of stitching
are years she blankets in dim remembering.

Every loop is a prayer of hand-locked yarn,
a protection from harm
till he parachutes home.

First Thanksgiving
Peggy Seely

Child bride, Navy pay
hundreds of miles from home.
Turkey day a week away

and all she's ever cooked:
grilled cheese, tomato soup,
scrambled eggs on Sunday.

She misses her mom, best cook
in town. Oh, no! Her mom
is coming for dinner with her

by Greyhound on Wednesday
right after work; won't arrive
in time to help or give advice.

For 35 cents Carnation had sent
a spiral-bound book of recipes.
She studies, stretches the budget,

buys the smallest turkey,
a whole pumpkin for pie,
condensed milk

and splurges on two tall candles.
The tablecloth was a wedding gift
with napkins that match.

At dinner-time on Thursday
it doesn't matter if the bird browned,
the coffee perked, the pie set

because sailing through the door
is her oh-so-new husband,
playing grown-up in his uniform,

whirling her in his arms,
laughing, "Surprise, honey!
My ship came in."

Fourth Grade Autobiography 1969
Heidi Nightengale

I.

We turned our papers up front, paper over head,
paper over head in automation. The kid with his name on an
owl that read, "teacher's assistant" on the daily job board
scurried to the front to collect them into a happy jumble of
something that I felt would be important. I didn't feel that way
about all my assignments. Next day, our papers were passed
back carefully by Mrs. Stinson, not the classroom owl assistant
from the job board. She walked each aisle and placed our papers
writing side down on each of our desks. "Students, you all have
more work to do. Turn over your papers, read my notes, begin
again."

II.

Mrs. Stinson's notes: (in red): *Good first draft. Revise.
Revise?* I was delighted to know I could *revise* my
autobiography! I started with a force that broke pencil tips
immediately. I did not wet my bed. I did not hate the red felt
coat with white piping that looked like a church coat and not a
school coat. I did not steal those cherry life savers when I was
five while my mother was busy with the check out lady at the
Red and White Market. In fact, I *had* to revise that because I
felt so bad about those lifesavers that I snuck them into the
outside trash burning barrel which only my father was allowed
to go near. I had not tasted one. I had not even opened them.
And I fought a feeling for years waiting to learn the word for
what that feeling was; it crawled up without call to curl and
tease its way into my stomach and mind. A feeling that swiped
my hunger.

But I *did* leave in the part about my drawings of the witch from
the "Fractured Fairy Tales." I could draw her plump, triangular
body, little trunk legs, and perfectly pointed hat (which I asked
for on every Christmas list). I was sure my drawings of her
looked just like she did on morning TV while I watched –one
eye on TV the other on the window for the bus. I drew her on
walls, my brother's desk, the back of my schoolwork papers,
my lunch bags, my new white Keds. I revised the part about

drawing her in a library book, though. That might save some
inquiries. I kept drawing her even after I heard my mother say to
my father, "She is still drawing those witches, Bob. Should we
be concerned? They are *witches.*" "Only if we find out she can
do magic," I heard my father reply in a voice that was not
preoccupied, not concerned. I hid behind the kitchen door and
listened in. I could always find a way to listen in and that seemed
a step in the magical direction.

III.

I didn't know how to revise the final part about my older brother
and his friends playing pool one June day near the end of third
grade. They were going to graduate. Some had something called
draft papers. My brother said he got his, too. I enjoyed their fun,
the nick names they had for each other: Monkey, Toe Joe, STP. I
didn't have to hide around them. They didn't care what I heard.
And sometimes they lifted me so I could shoot at the white cue
ball toward any ball they thought I could get into a pocket. They
let me cue up their sticks. Monkey said he knew a guy already
who was in Vietnam and his sister said his letters home were all
about cool things he was doing. My oldest brother and the others
with these papers all gave hand slaps until my mother walked into
the game room.

My mother was beautiful walking into that room. It must have
been close to the time my father got home because her hair was
curled and her lipstick was on. She was always the most
beautiful when she was waiting for my father. She told me to scat
and ordered the boys to follow her to the kitchen. I dragged
upstairs to my room but then stealthed right back down and found
a perfect hiding spot under the dining room buffet. My mother
said, "If you want to see cool things that you will be doing in
Vietnam, look at this."

She reached for a magazine on the top of the refrigerator. The
magazine was passed from boy to boy, none of them hand
slapping. None of them even speaking. I heard STP speak first.
"Sorry, Mrs. Nightengale." I heard my brother say he was sorry,
too. And then the magazine was put back out of reach and I heard
my mother tell them not to let the little kids get their hands on
this. But I did. When the coast was clear I drew chair to counter
and climbed the counter to my eyes' view of the top of the
refrigerator. It was a *Life* magazine. Pages still folded out showed

naked girls running. I think they were on fire. I think they were
my age. That lifesaver feeling crawled back into by belly. I got
down without noise, replaced the chair, and joined everyone in
the living room for Animal Kingdom. I passed on the popcorn.

IV.

My oldest brother worked a few days after school at the milk
bottling plant. One night during dinner, a few days after I
sneaked to the top of the refrigerator, the phone rang. It was for
my Dad.   My brother had been hurt. "How hurt?" dad said. He
repeated the answer and the rest of the conversation back to my
mother as if the rest of us were not at the table. "He has cut off his
finger. His trigger finger. That's it then. He's not going. The
supervisor says it is a mystery. The guards had been checked.
They were all up. This shouldn't have happened. The guard rails
were checked and up." I managed a scoop of corn thinking the
"Fractured Fairy Tale" witch that I drew on that *Life* magazine to
protect the running girls, to help them find their mothers may
have played some magic for my brother, too.

Be Positive
Katie Turner

Be positive
they say
when he calls
don't speak of
the car repairs
the children's struggles
at school
the water-leak
in the basement
or how
your mother
now has cancer

Be positive
they say
I speak
of the birds
in the yard
the horseradish, zucchini
growing in the garden
the call from your sister

Be positive
they tell you
you speak of the cities
you've seen
the interpreters
you've met
the letters you've received

Be positive
they tell you
don't speak
of the
morning ice mortars
that wake your FOB
the up-armored truck
exploding in front of you
the way you chased the enemy through streets
how you now

wear your weapon
everywhere
or how it surprises you
how deep and wide
loneliness
can be

Be positive
they say
I hear secrets behind your words
you tell me you are safe
how U.S. soldiers are
the best trained
still fears float thickly
unaddressed
they grow
and fester
like a hideous imaginary creature
until I receive
your next call

Be positive
they tell me

A Washing Machine in Air Force Housing
Dean C. Dickinson

In the spring of 1963, my wife and I had been living for over a year in government housing at Ramstein Air Base in Germany. There were twenty-four families in our four-story building. As a Lieutenant I was assigned to an apartment on the top floor. There was, of course, no elevator. We had a small daughter, and my wife was expecting our second child. Those were the days of cloth diapers, and we did a lot of laundry. The washers and dryers were in the basement and that meant going up and down four flights of stairs for each load of wash. If the machines were already in use, as they often were, that meant even more vertical travel. When my wife learned some of the residents had washing machines hooked up in their kitchens, she wanted me to get one for us. That seemed like an excellent idea so I bought one from a family that was moving back to the states and had it delivered to our apartment. Then I was con-fronted with the problem of getting it hooked up to our kitchen faucet.

My wife helpfully suggested I call the building maintenance office and ask them to install it. But I knew how slow those guys reacted to any requests for help, and I wanted to get this thing working right away. So, I decided to take matters into my own hands—I wasn't going to wait around for anybody. Of course, I realized I faced several problems going it alone on this. First of all, I knew absolutely nothing about plumbing. Second, all of the water turn-off valves were located somewhere in the basement, but they were not marked and could not be easily identified. Third, any tampering with the water supply to my kitchen might well have an undesirable effect on some of the other tenants (including a number of higher-ranking officers). I figured I could handle each of these problems with a little careful planning and resourcefulness.

I went to a German hardware store and bought a selection of cast iron pipefittings and a couple of wrenches. I sketched out a modification of the kitchen faucet that I thought would provide a convenient hookup for the washer. It looked awkward, but I figured it would serve the purpose. I wondered about how best to make the various connections watertight and decided to use a heavy black goop I had used as a sealant on my car. I planned to do the installation on an evening when my wife was not home. I wanted to surprise her.

Locating the correct water turn-off valve was a complicated problem. I started by turning the kitchen faucet on full force so I could hear it from the hallway entrance. Then I went down the four flights of stairs to the basement, picked a valve at random, shut it off, ran back up the steps to my open doorway and listened for the faucet. It was still running. So, I ran down to the basement, turned that valve back on and tried turning another one off. I flew back up the stairs at a run, but again no success. These valves were not lined up in order—they were all over the place. I continued trekking up and down those endless stairs trying every valve I could find. I almost gave up before I finally located the right one. All the time I was rushing up and down the stairs, past all those other apartments, I dreaded the moment someone would open their door and ask me what I was doing. Several times I thought I heard a door open on a floor above or below me and I froze for a moment until I could tell the coast was clear. Even after I found the right valve my worries were not over. I couldn't be sure I wasn't turning someone else's water off too. The last thing I needed was some irate Colonel in a towel accusing me of scalding him in his shower.

When I finally got the water shut off, I quickly went to work with my German tools and my supply of fittings. I applied the black goop liberally and screwed my contrivance together as tightly as I could. Then I left the door open again and ran down to turn the pressure back on. By now I was sweaty, anxious and winded from all that strenuous exercise but I had to keep hurrying in my race against the clock. When I stumbled back up the steps for what I hoped was the last time I could hear the hissing and splattering of escaping water before I even reached the landing. I dashed into the kitchen and was amazed to see a gigantic fountain spraying across the entire room. The black goop was all over the walls and floor and was even plastered onto the ceiling. With a sickening feeling of dismay and defeat I raced back to the basement and turned the pressure off. Then I ran panting back upstairs and worked desperately to put the original faucet back together. I held my breath as I turned the basement valve back on and ran up to the kitchen to see if it was holding the pressure. I gave a giant sigh of relief when I saw there were no leaks this time. Then I hustled to try and clean up all that black goop before my wife returned. I was afraid she would walk in and get a real surprise.

When I told her all about my evening's activities, she again suggested I call the maintenance people and ask them to do it the right way. I agreed, but with a sense of foreboding that we would probably get the machine working about the time we were ready to move back to the states. So, the next day I made the dreaded phone call. I simply told them I had bought a washing machine and asked if they would install it for me. But then I was astonished when the desk sergeant said, "Sure thing sir, I'll send someone over tomorrow afternoon and we'll get that hooked right up for you." And they did.

Red Sun/White Silk

Maureen Teresa McCarthy

Snapshots tumble from a cardboard box on a high shelf
Pale faces stare up at me from the closet floor
Smiling men in far places, solemn mothers and shy children
Who are these people? Do I know them?

Boats I've never sailed, coastlines never seen
Stairways never climbed
There is another life here. Why am I saving it?
Instead of my own?

Orders – typed on onionskin
Wrapped in a square of pale silk, centered with a red sun
The Japanese flag
And I am pure Celt

More silk – a kimono richly shaded in gorgeous colors
Pink and cream, green, lavender
My colors, but this was my father's war
Why is it in my closet?

In the sleeve, another photo – the teahouse
Two soldiers in khaki sit on bamboo mats
A low table, perfectly set
One round pot, three cups, one orchid

A lovely woman stands in a flowered kimono
Is it the same one I hold in my hands?
I will never know.
The fabric glows.

Atonal Memories
Janet Fagal

My father climbs the ladder
higher and higher
in his black Hawaiian shirt,
not yet a fashion trend in the fifties.
Now high above the crowd
lights from the portable bandstand
gleam against a darkened sky.

Music soars in the night.
My father and his trumpet singing.
Bright and burnished,
they call to the crowd.

Melodies blaze and pulse
in piercing tones.
Pure and centered.
Vibrant like fire.
Cool like crystal.
Two separate souls,
the trumpet and my father,
now merged and dancing.
A genius and a horn.

The crowd sways
to the music pouring forth
like fireworks in summer.
Memories made in melodies
drift on the summer air
of my childhood.

Too soon the music dies.
The last words I ever spoke to my father
were not about the gifts of music.
Nor words of thanks.
The last words I ever spoke to my father
were ordinary, almost cold.

If could see him climb
the ladder again,
I would listen this time
with my whole heart.
Gaze at the air
with a reverence he could taste,
and lose myself in the
soul of his trumpet.

Pure metal
made whole and alive.
By my father's lips,
By my father's smile.

After my grandmother passed away, my mother loaded all the stuff from the attic and basement of her childhood home into a U-haul and dumped it in her garage for sorting. I was invited to help sort through the forgotten treasures and amongst the boxes of family photos, old shoes, and the accumulated knick-knacks was a treasure few ever see. In an ugly canvas bag, dyed the most obnoxious shades of blue and bright green "fashionable" in the late 60's, were a pile of letters. Upon inspection, I discovered that the letters were a correspondence between my mother and father when he was in the Navy.

Dad and Mom had gotten married right after boot camp. Mom had discovered she was pregnant while he was in basic training. Dad was home for my birth and christening but was deployed when I was less than two months old. Mom lived with Dad's family in a small in-law apartment in the basement of the house, as she was back in school to finish her senior year. They hadn't let her attend school once she started to show, even though she was married.

The letters began in September 1967 and continued through the first half of the following year. My grandmother had saved the letters from both Mom and Dad, and I carefully put them in chronological order and sat down to read them. Dad's ship, U.S.S. Mississinewa, was cruising the Med refueling ships headed to Vietnam. Dad had joined the Navy Reserves while his brother, Don, had joined the Army. Service was expected in their family. Grandpa had been in the Air Force in WWII and Grandma had worked as a secretary in Washington D.C. for the FBI.

Dad's letters invariably began with questions about me and went on to describe the mundane aspects of living on an oil tanker, he never wrote her of anything frightening or disturbing. In nearly all Dad's letters he asks about how much money was in the bank account. He sent money home regularly so that they could save for a home of their own when he got out of the service. On the back of every envelope were the numbers 1 4 3.

Mom's responses were often filled with normal teenage drama about my aunt's borrowing her clothes and not returning them or things happening at school. She always wrote about the current bank balance and her after school job at the grocery. Sometimes she wrote about the trials and tribulations of motherhood, how much she missed him, and how much I was growing. Dad learned of me crawling and saying my first words in those letters.

On the back of the envelopes were lip stains in pale pink and S.W.A.K. (sealed with a kiss)

After reading through a handful of the letters I asked Mom about the numbers on the back of the envelope. I could not figure out what they meant. They did not correspond to any of the family addresses. Mom laughed and told me it was code. The numbers related to the number of letters in each of the words "I" "Love" "You." My father had never been a demonstrative man, he "kept himself to himself" most of the time and this seemed perfectly in character. Although Dad didn't often tell us he loved us, we all felt it. Those letters are still bundled in that ugly canvas bag, buried in a closet, a hidden treasure for his grandchildren to rediscover.

Just Another War Story
Peggy Seely

He walks away; I do not see him anymore.
I rail against the cruel demands of war.
At night, my pillow cannot hold my tears
nor platitudes alleviate my fears.
How many untried prayers to chant before

he's safe. I can't imagine what's in store.
This separation cuts me to the core.
When battles rage, relentless, throughout years,
he walks away,

returns to me, but they are keeping score.
He has no choice when they come to the door.
Life is death when all hope disappears.
No marching home amid triumphant cheers.
In dreams I see this boy I still adore.
He walks away.

Uncle Sergeant
Kimberly Slaughter-Cunningham

Lean build, hair parted to the side, strong work ethics and good morals made Uncle Sergeant very respectable. Often times he ate meals with us, enjoying more than one plate of delicious home cooked food. Avid fisherman and sometimes hunter, occasional frog leg catcher, he spent lots of time exploring our stretched-out acres of our dairy farm in rural NY. Funny stories, and songs were always happening when he was around. Small child that I was, got excited each time he drew near. I sat next to him, followed him, asked thousands of questions of which he answered every single one.

A favorite memory of being with Uncle Sergeant is from a windy, 70 something degree Summer day. I had a bat shaped kite that I gotten from the local Woolworth's store. He came to our home and told me to get the kite. Together we walked up a hill in the field behind the house. My uncle showed me how to get the kite in the air and how to guide it. I learned how to make dips and dives and follow the wind patterns. I was delighted. Yet, in the five year old mind I had, I was worried about being pulled up in the air as the kite went higher and higher. He told me not to be scared because he would protect me and nothing would happen.

Uncle Sergeant is a great human being, he had a way of making people feel safe. I always wanted to keep him in close proximity. However, things were getting difficult in our home-land, and Uncle Sergeant had to make some hard choices. Soon he wouldn't be so near anymore. The country was involved in the Viet Nam war and it would be his time to get the call. Uncle Sergeant decided to sign up for the Army, instead of waiting. Just like that, he got his orders to report for basic training, then Uncle Sergeant was gone. Mom said he would be back for visits and he would write. He left a void that was never filled. Looking out the windows for him frequently, I was hoping he could come back to us quickly. Pieces of mail came with pictures of Uncle Sergeant in his uniform. Looking clean and crisp, Uncle Sergeant stood tall. Both of my parents said he was brave. My entire family worried about him, especially since there was a war going on.

Letters came often and we read about his new life. Mom sat and cried. Phone rang and it was Uncle Sergeant with a short call to tell us about what was going on. He said he would be headed overseas for a long period of time. Mom cried more than before. Pictures of his Army life, calls about new cousins being born, written pages full of details with air mail stamps on them all became part of our lives. He sent tape recordings to my grandfather and we went to his house to listen to what Uncle Sergeant had to say. There was a mixture of feelings about him being gone so far away. Proudness combined with worry seemed to be the consensus among the adults. As for me, I just wanted to see my uncle again. When Uncle Sergeant was able come for a visit, there was excitement in the air. Big parties happened and he told us of his experiences. There was lots of music, laughter, food at the gatherings. Everyone wanted to be near Uncle Sergeant. Those were happy times, they were the best of times. Sadly, more than once we went to the airport to send Uncle Sergeant back to Germany. Mom shed more tears.

Over the years we sent lots of letters and received piles of letters. Eventually, my uncle wrote to tell us that he was promoted from PFC to Sergeant status. Another picture came, this time it was of him getting his advancement. In addition, we learned of life on a military base in another country from those writings. Each time a letter came from him, I ran from the mailbox to my mother so we could tear it open and read it. Sometimes gifts were sent as well. When things got really special, he came home for Christmas once or twice. Wonderful times, happy times when he was around. Always followed by sadness though when he had to depart yet another time. Uncle Sergeant was dedicated to and committed to serving his country, so he left.

Uncle Sergeant served 20 years of his life in the Army. Towards the end of his service, he was a recruiter. It was his way of giving to the future and selecting quality candidates to serve our country. As he ended his time, he was a career military man ready to return home at that point. Retirement for him meant coming back and building a house for his family. Longing for his own acres to roam and a place for his children, Uncle Sergeant came to stay with us again, so he could get established.

Eventually, he bought a big property and brought his family from the military housing where they lived in the Southern US, to the new residence in NY state. By then I was out on my own but came to visit as often as I could. I still felt the excitement of seeing him. Mom had finally stopped crying and felt joyous.

Uncle Sergeant was here to stay! He worked at a few jobs 'til he settled in as an animal control peace officer. As an adult now, I really understand what his service meant and know the greatness of what he did in his life. Following in his footsteps, his youngest son served in the Army, doing a tour in Iraq and one in Afghanistan as an 82nd Airborne Paratrooper and two of his grandsons are currently In the Army. He had made an impact on their lives and they chose to serve in part because of him. True men of bravery, all of them.

I salute my Uncle Sergeant.

Broken
Janet Fagal

She sees his face,
a picture etched
in memory.
Her child's image.
Eyes dark,
piercing.
Nose strong.
Mouth full,
hints of smile.
She hears his voice.
The sounds: low wails,
whimpers.
Her son
frightened by bombs,
watches
through rubble
and smoke.
Again and again the
roar of war
sends them running.
New shelter.
Cramped hovel,
temporary.
The necessaries: food, water, hope,
too limited.
A hand,
rough, calloused
reaches out.
Safety,
come.
A gesture,
the truck readies.
Room for one.
She pushes her son,
up.
A mother's heart
shatters.

Another Happy Camper © 2004 Frank Light

Nesh District, northern Kandahar province in Afghanistan This was taken on the camera I was carrying, most likely* by an infantryman from Bravo Company with the 2/5 battalion of the 25th Infantry Division or possibly by the battalion surgeon or one of two MPs from the Provincial Reconstruction Team who traveled with us.

this photo does not necessarily represent the positions of the United States Government.

FROM JUNGLE TO DESERT

A Phone in the Jungle
Laurie Kolp

While trudging through Panama, trying to oust
Noriega during Operation Just Cause,
Pete and his men stood on guard
carefully sneaking through dense woods,
staving off scorpions, snakes, leeches and ticks
not to mention body fungus and bothersome mosquitoes
that attacked in dark of night, leaving chicken pox welts
on men from up North, men with sensitive skin.
All the Marines tired, hungry, in need of showers.
Spirits plummeting with each left-right-left rhythm
of soggy boots. Until they saw it: a tattered gray box
standing on a pole all alone in the middle of the jungle.
Quick glance skyward revealed a wire leading
somewhere through the trees. Being the brave hero
that he was, Pete stepped up to container, opened it
(thank God it was not a bomb). Sitting right there
as plain as the enemy was an old telephone.
Everyone dropped their jaws and looked at Pete.
He stepped up to the plate, lifted the receiver to his ear
and heard the low monotone *bbbbbbbbbb*
old phones make. Pete dialed O and waited for a response.
"Operator. Can I help you?" said a nasally voice.
"Uh... yeah. I'd like to make a collect call," Pete spit out.
He gave her a number off the top of his head.
A few rings, Pete's father answered phone, said hello.
After rigmarole of saying his name and waiting
for his dad to accept the call, they were able to talk
and NO, he was not in jail. All the other guys used
the phone to call their loved ones. Then they marched
forward in unison, new springs in staunch steps.

A Reflection from the Gulf War
Penny Lee Deere

The year,1990, the buildup "Desert Storm."
Thanksgiving and Christmas eating sand, breathing smoke.
A new year, 1991, brings "Desert Shield."
For 42 consecutive days,
Six weeks of airstrikes,
Over 100,000 sorties prior to the ground war,
As the oil fuels burned, lit on fire,
We pounded them with air suppression,
Smart bombs with massive payloads.
You see they pick on the little guy.
They invaded Kuwait, tried to annex this county
  Make it theirs. "Oh no"
This is unacceptable to the other 39 nations that came
to the rescue.

One hundred hours of ground war--three days it was over.
As I pulled guard duty in the makeshift bunker—
  a foxhole, in a berm, sandbags lining the walls—
My M16 ready and M60 on board,
It seemed like Independence Day back home
bombs bursting in air .
—The streaks, the explosions can be seen for miles.
—The smells drifted.
—The light show was magnificent.

The aftermath—too much—
War stinks.
Now to live with the guilt,
I, the targeteer, responsible for all that destruction

Cold Steel, Bobcats, and BUBs
Frank Light

1970-72 I was a Peace Corps volunteer in Afghanistan. The first year I taught English as a foreign language in a village outside Jalalabad. In 2003, I returned for three months as the State Department representative to a start-up Provincial Reconstruction Team, or PRT, in that town. A pilot project, we were told to enhance security, extend the reach of the national government, and promote development. As the sole civilian, I brought an outside perspective to those of my military colleagues. Our complement never exceeded 25, and we covered – tried to cover – three provinces. Fertile ground. Conversations with villagers, officials, and aid workers allowed me to report on areas little known to Kabul, Bagram, and Washington. The civil affairs Reservists who comprised the rest of the team contributed unique skills and approaches to the larger American effort.

Family obligations limited my tour, though as it turned out wife and daughter did fine on their own. After a few months together, me on leave without pay to accommodate my wife's position at our embassy in Copenhagen, I looked into PRT openings for 2004. Positive reviews from 2003 led to their proliferation throughout the country.

My first choice was a new one north of Jalalabad in Kunar, where an otherwise all-Afghan team and I had initiated food-for-work projects my second year in the Peace Corps. But the position was filled, as was the one I'd vacated in Jalalabad. I asked about Bamiyan, where my wife and I first met (on the Buddha the Taliban later blew up). Already accounted for. Before Kunar I did similar work at the other end of the country, in Farah. My new first choice. They're not ready for State, I was told.

The State desk faced a more pressing problem – no volunteers for three proto-PRTs in the old Taliban dust belt where the Pentagon did want State officers. Supply couldn't keep up with demand. Afghanistan was last year's hot spot. Saddam had replaced Osama as public enemy number one, and the sound of the guns combined with the chance to make history and money and boost (or salvage) a career while at it proved irresistible to the young, newly divorced, true-believers, and the ambitious. For others – Arabic speakers, for example – duty (and senior officials) called.

Our aid agency resorted to contractors, State to retirees, civil servants, and interns, to staff PRTs in the northern half of Afghanistan. Not counting Farah, and State certainly wasn't, the only PRTs it couldn't find anybody to go to were in Khost, Zabul, and Uruzgan provinces.

Khost could surprise, the desk advised; gets better all the time. Too close to Kabul for my tastes. Also, we had infantry there. The PRT would be a sideshow. Same in Zabul, astride the Kabul-Kandahar highway the U.S. had repaved to great fanfare. North of Zabul and Kandahar, Uruzgan lay in nobody's path. Neither encyclopedias nor old guidebooks mentioned it, and even Google had little to offer.

I knew only that Taliban Supreme Leader Mullah Omar came from there and was last seen heading that direction when he high-tailed it from Kandahar in December 2001. The month before, a U.S. helicopter inserted president-in-waiting Karzai into Uruzgan, and the air strikes his Special Forces escort called on a Taliban reaction force broke their backs for good.

Our Special Forces subsequently moved from Tarin Kot, the provincial capital, to western Uruzgan. That left a hole the future PRT could fill. Sign me up, I said. Make it a year, the desk responded. I held my ground. Everything being equal, I would have given them what they wanted. Lord knows I owed it. But my wife was putting in long hours, and our only child was a teenager in a foreign land. State finally agreed to take me for their minimum, my maximum – 90 days starting August, same as in Jalalabad.

That spring the Marines established a beachhead near Tarin Kot. They named it Forward Operating Base Ripley after a hero, still living, from the Vietnam War. One of their number and about a hundred Afghans died in the ensuing skirmishes. A long way from the water, the Marines weren't going to stay more than a few months. It was unclear if they'd be replaced. I crossed my fingers. The PRT would be enough, in my view. A province that needed a maneuver unit wasn't ready for a PRT. The Pentagon must have thought otherwise, for it sent the 2nd Battalion of the 5th Regiment, 25th Infantry Division – the 2/5, they called themselves – to replace the Marines. The much smaller PRT co-located with them at Ripley. I was concerned about sharing a base – and a province – with the infantry, which we didn't have in Jalalabad. Although their presence seemed to comfort the PRT in Tarin Kot, it made me apprehensive. They had numbers, logistics, firepower, and money. The Afghans would listen to them, not the PRT.

My experience with the military had mostly been on the fringes of Special Forces – a year as an auditor for the 5th Group in Vietnam, three years desk-jockeying with Special Operations on a detail to the Pentagon, and three months in a compound the PRT shared with an operational detachment in Jalalabad. My only sightings of the infantry, apart from officers doing time in that puzzle palace by the Potomac, had been in Vietnam. The guys I ran into there looked haunted, dogged. Secretary Rumsfeld claimed conscripts provided "no value" for that war, implying they weren't in uniform long enough and weren't buying into the program when the reality is they paid the price for lock-step leadership. Despite the talk of hearts and minds, it was body counts that registered. A more fundamental mistake: there were too many of us. At home, the cost in blood and treasure became unsustainable. In South Vietnam, we overwhelmed the culture, economy, and initiative. The mindset became – let the Americans do it; we'll get out of it what we can.

I feared we were doing a similar thing in Afghanistan – sending the infantry, upping the ante. Not smart, maybe, but it showed resolve – with limits. Repeating another flaw from our Vietnam misadventure, we left the enemy a sanctuary. Two major differences – this time the world was on our side, and ending the draft made it politically easier to send more soldiers for a longer time. 9/11 triggered a mandate. This was the necessary war, the small war, the un-Iraq. But our increasing numbers begged the bottom-line question: what happens after the boys come home? If we nurtured resentments as we suppressed resistance, we would have merely postponed the reckoning. We would have left our enemies more determined, our allies sapped.

As appropriate for a maneuver unit, the 2/5 got around. It operated for several months in Ghazni before deploying (minus a platoon in Kabul) to Uruzgan. It posted a platoon with the Special Forces and Afghan National Army at a firebase west of Tarin Kot. Later on, Charlie Company would open a firebase north of there while Alpha manned one to the east. Only Bravo and headquarters elements worked out of Ripley.

Their mascot was the bobcat; their commanding officer, a lieutenant colonel, used "Bobcat 6" as his call sign. Not sure of what my association should be with such an outfit, I asked to meet him soon after my arrival. A State guy had been with the PRT in Ghazni, so Bobcat 6 had an idea what he was getting. He invited me to his daily battle update briefing, or BUB, rhymes with tub, that the PRT commander or executive officer also attended. Officers and senior sergeants occupied folding chairs arranged in rows on a plywood platform under a large tent, with standing room for the lower ranks in the back.

A wiry, bespectacled hard-charger who had started his military career as a Marine Reservist until he won an appointment to West Point, Bobcat 6 sat in the front row, king of the court, arms tucked, legs crossed, as captains and sergeants took turns briefing him. If they had a problem, they knew to report it early and to include what they were doing to resolve it. Any whiff of procrastination, he bored in like a prosecuting attorney. When, on the other hand, there was progress, he'd crack a joke. A captain or major would throw out another. Everybody looked for reasons to laugh.

He thought about things but never hesitated. That would be so un-Army. He didn't mince words, and his voice was, shall I say, crisp. Yet he was always polite and restrained with me, perhaps at first because I had a separate chain of command that lent me an aura, at least until he and his staff realized my agency didn't reach that far into the weeds, later because he saw I wasn't going to give away the family secrets and we agreed on what should be done. He acceded to every request but my last – to accompany soldiers clearing new ground – for support.

Every day he had to fight for his own support. He bulldogged, bulldozed, bullwhipped, bullshitted, bamboozled, badgered, berated, befriended, whatever it took, to get the aerial surveillance, intelligence, IED jammers, airlift, vehicle parts, weaponry, generators, specialists, construction equipment, and anything else necessary to get the job done. He didn't always succeed, and he rubbed some the wrong way, as the 2/5 wasn't the only unit experiencing shortages. Iraq had something to do with that. But as with any dispersed organization, there was also inertia, routine, cynicism, accidents, mistakes, distractions, grudges, buck-passing, metal, mental, and physical fatigue, faulty assumptions, failures to connect dots, a bigger down than upside to exercises in judgment, the learned experience that you'd be a fool not to take care of yourself first when everybody else was, and a self-preservationist drive to hold something back for a real emergency, like when a general called.

Having picked up some lessons from Vietnam, the command understood that campaigns equated to more than the sum of their firefights. I don't think everyone down the chain internalized it, however. Combat arms drew stand-up guys who saw force as the answer and sometimes even the question. Bobcat 6 had those tendencies. He kept them in check. He kept his men in check. The officers under him were as careful about calling in artillery and air support, with its potential for "collateral damage," as they were about minimizing risks to their own men. Unlike in Vietnam, the troopers kept to the straight and narrow. They knew not to fool with the women. There was no alcohol to lead them astray. If caught with drugs, you were gone.

Attitudes and language were harder to police. These men were, after all, grunts. Throughout the theater soldiers used "haji" to mean any Afghan. A term of respect in the local culture, the honorific for a man who had made the pilgrimage, it was a dismissive word in ours, like "slope" or "gook" in Vietnam. He had no tolerance for it.

The PRT often escorted me to meetings in Tarin Kot. In September we visited a former comrade of the Governor's in their jihad against the Soviets. Lacking tribal connections, this veteran's reward was an adobe office with half a roof, dirt for a floor, no door for the doorway, and nothing for its occupant to do as provincial Director of Energy. Electricity originated only from small, building-specific generators that ran for a few hours in the evening. To address the shortfall our aid mission sent a generator sized for municipal use but no funds, fuel, or means to connect it to anything. It sat outside his office. Still a rebel at heart, he chafed at the way things were. While he vented, my escort flushed peekaboo eyes from an abandoned building next door. Boys ran away laughing. What else would we do but laugh too?

From there we drove to the Governor's palace, checking to see if he was back. It had been months. No news. So we went to see about his rival, the Chief of Police, also absent for months. Again, no news. Neither had a real deputy. My escorts used the occasion to persuade the few cops on duty to let us confiscate the marijuana from a garden they tended inside the front gate.

On the drive back a PRT turret gunner spied a man with a machine gun on a rooftop. Each gun trained on the other. The PRT reported this to the 2/5. Consistent with the agreed division of labor, Charlie Company headed downtown to investigate.

At the BUB that afternoon Bobcat 6 announced Bravo Company had created a video to mark the third anniversary of the 9/11 attacks. I had almost forgotten. You could do that here. In Jalalabad it had been a training day. The video showed familiar footage of the telescoping towers and the Pentagon in flames. Flags waved, music played, and the 2/5 sprang into action on the screen, emphasis on hard travels and helping hands rather than guns a-blazing. When it was over, the assemblage both somber and inspired, the colonel sprang to his feet a second time to ask if anybody had been in the Pentagon that day. Only I raised a hand. He said he'd been there, too.

That led to a silence reminiscent of the corridors after the initial evacuation. Smoke there, dust here. Charlie Company's commander lightened the mood with a recitation of the contraband his men had seized in the building with the machine gun on top – a conex full of rocket launchers and mines, devices for triggering those mines, twenty cases of grenades, three mortar tubes, two light machine guns counting the one on the roof, one anti-aircraft gun, 300 AK-47s, ammunition for the preceding, a packet of blank voter registration cards, and sixty kilos of opium paste. The house militia were not happy about it, although they offered no resistance. They said they worked for the Governor.

A 2/5 sergeant entered from stage right. After pausing for a catch-up breath and a nod from the colonel to go ahead, he announced the Governor was back and wanted to see Bobcat 6 right away. Bobcat 6 flashed a smile you could slice salami with. He said he'd go in the morning.

The PRT commander spoke up. His interpreter had told him about the Governor's return and arranged for the commander's farewell call the next morning. The two colonels decided they would go together, Bobcat 6 to hear what was on the Governor's mind, and then the PRT commander could pay his respects. The colonels were proper with each other but there was no bonhomie. I asked the PRT commander if he would introduce me to the Governor. He agreed, so I rode with him.

The PRT was my principle support, primarily through civil affairs and headquarters components relieved "in place" after lengthy gaps and an ever-present company from the 168th Infantry of the Iowa National Guard. When the PRT commander entered the tent for our own BUB, the Guardsmen snapped to attention and barked "Cold Steel!" Promoting development in a "non-permissive" environment was no easy task. Rifle in one hand, other out in greeting, the PRT was more than up to it.

I also availed myself of the 2/5's clout, hospitality, and reach. Bobcat 6 and I often attended the Governor's office, the battalion's fire-control officer and I collaborated on the presidential election, and I journeyed to the districts with Alpha and Bravo Companies as well as with the PRT. I admired the soldiers' efficiency, spirit, and sense of the other. At my last 2/5 BUB I said that coming in I reckoned the battalion could handle the Taliban. I hadn't expected they would be equally adept at diplomacy. Indeed, several officers had asked about openings at State, and I'd told them about a Pentagon colleague who joined the Foreign Service on retiring from command of a Special Forces battalion. Last I heard, he was in Iraq. I said if they thought my job looked cool – travel the world while others did your dirty work – they should know our embassies and Foggy Bottom weren't nearly as much fun as Uruzgan. That drew a few smiles. But I offered no knee-slappers. It didn't seem right, and it wasn't in my nature.

Military officers generally project better than Foreign Service Officers like me who are more comfortable doing it in writing.

They are especially adept at using humor to mask emotion in farewell remarks. Standing in front of them, I felt the pressure of high expectations. I reminded them of that which they already knew but rarely talked about: extending security to this country provided it for our own. They were more than competent. They were smart. That was the infantry's great secret.

*** *This does not necessarily represent the positions of the United States Government.*

Aboard the Maloy
Thomas Seely

In late June of 1950, my graduation from high school in Trumansburg, New York coincided with news of something big happening at the 38th Parallel in a far-off and little-known part of the world called Korea. At seventeen, I had no plan for my future or even a clear image of what I wanted to do with it. Along with some of my buddies, I goofed the summer away, fishing, swimming, going to the local movie on Friday nights, attending street dances in the middle of town on Saturday nights.

My part-time jobs, pin-setter at the bowling alley, stable hand for the Smiths, paid enough to treat my girl-friend to milk-shakes at Malone's Drugstore a couple of times a week. As the days slipped by, talk of war surrounded us, and by September, I had decided to follow the example of my two older brothers to enter the military. Charlie spent his World War II years fighting on Guam, Ted was a Medic in DC, eventually sent to New Zealand. The lure of adventure claimed me, and, just as they did, I joined the United States Navy.

I experienced my first train ride on the trip from Buffalo, New York to Newport, Rhode Island. The Naval base at Newport had just been reopened as a Boot Camp. I was one of 120 men in Company 7. We spent eleven weeks training and learning the basics of Navy life. Upon completion, the other men from my Company were sent to the West coast to board ships headed for Korea. For reasons I'll never understand I was assigned to the USS Maloy EDE791 in New London, Connecticut. EDE stood for Experimental Destroyer Escort.

When I got to the Maloy, I was put in the deck gang. These were the guys handling the mooring lines as we got under weigh and as we docked. At Battle stations we manned the guns. My station was as the pointer on a twin 40 MM machine gun. While in port, the deck gang was responsible for the maintenance and cleaning of much of the ship which included swabbing the decks and chipping and painting the super-structure. While at sea, we stood watches, four hours on and eight hours off. My duty station was as the bridge talker who communicated with the port, starboard, bow and stern watches using a sound powered phone. Any information from these stations was given to the Captain or Officer of the Deck on the bridge, which, onboard ship, is the center of navigation. The Maloy had an open flying bridge directly over the pilot house and the Combat Information Center. At sea there were usually three people on the bridge: the Officer of the Deck, a Quartermaster and the bridge talker. The pilot house needed three people, the helmsman, the enunciator operator and the keeper of the ship's log. In CIC were the radar, radio and sonar operators. I transferred to "O" [operations] division and was sent to Quartermaster school in Bainbridge, Maryland. School consisted of a seven week course covering all aspects of navigation and signaling.

Soon after returning to the Maloy from QM school I passed the tests and became a rated Quartermaster. At sea, the Quartermaster confirms the ship's location using sightings of known objects when in sight of land. When out of sight of land the ship's position can be shown using Loran, a system which receives radio signals from stations to show position. Sun and star sightings using a sextant are also used to verify position. Accurate time is totally essential to navigation when you are out of sight of land. I became the person responsible for the Chart House where our three chronometers were located, set in gimbles in an enclosed case to keep them level regardless of the ship's motion. They had to be wound daily and compared to Greenwich mean time with any variation recorded. When the ship's exact position was required, a stopwatch was activated using a chronometer reading corrected to the variation to give a precise time. Sextant readings are as accurate as possible to show the ship's position.

My major responsibility in the chart house was to assure that all charts and publications were up to date for the areas in which we would be sailing. This gave those in "O" division an advantage in that we knew where we were going before the rest of the crew.

While on watch at sea, my station was on the flying bridge recording our location on charts so I could recommend course changes to the Officer of the Deck to avoid hazards and other vessels. The Officer of the Deck would give orders for course and speed changes through a voice tube between the bridge and pilot house. The helmsman would acknowledge by repeating the order back to the Officer of the deck. If the order was for a change in heading, the helmsman would make that change. If the order was for a change in speed, that information was sent to the engine room by the enunciator. When all orders had been complied with, the helmsman would let the Officer of the Deck know through the voice tube.

Most of our time at sea was on daily operations working with submarines. Our ship had a variable depth sonar unit mounted on the port side. We often had scientists from Woods Hole on board experimenting with the VDS. There is a thermal layer in the ocean that blocks normal sonar, thus a submarine under that layer could be undetected. With VDS we were able to lower the transducer below that layer and locate submarines.

Upon entering or leaving port, at Battle stations, and at special sea detail, my station was at the helm. When the tides were running, maintaining the heading was much more difficult. You've heard the expression "flying by the seat of his pants". Well, I could sense somehow when we were about to go off course. Naturally, I had the compass at hand, but sometimes when I knew it wouldn't create a problem, I would see how long the ship would travel before I had to change the rudder. This exercise was frowned upon.

We docked at the submarine base in New London, Connecticut; to get there it was necessary to pass through a narrow opening in a Bascule railroad bridge. The Captain would not announce a specific heading but would tell me "take 'er her through" and I did.

One time I had just nicely settled in for a liberty weekend when a knock on the door announced two members of shore patrol saying that I was the only rated Quartermaster they could find from the Maloy. I had to go with them so that the ship could get underway to avoid an on-coming hurricane! I had never done the navigation to get the ship out into open waters but had observed it many times. Luckily, we made it safely to the sound, dropped anchor and rode out the storm.

Looking back from my 86th year, I realize I enjoyed my time in the Navy, saw interesting places, had some memorable experiences, but I'm content that I decided against making it my career.

Army Nurse
Mike Dailey

Chutes floating over the jungle
Must have been about mid-day
And when shadows moved in the evening
We would lie in our cots and pray
The red sun on the canopy
Told us who they were
No time to think about them
Our days are such a blur
A tent isn't much protection
When the enemy comes to call
We'd hear a shout or a gun shot
Curl up in a foxhole ball
Sleep still in our khakis
A helmet by our bed
Roll ourselves under the tent flap
And sleep on the ground instead
A rosary in my pocket
A prayer upon my tongue
A letter still in writing
From a nurse that felt so young
In the daylight, see the damage
From a night that felt so long
Scrub up for the morning duty
Let the soldiers see you're strong
They carry them in on stretchers
Or in the backseat of a jeep
This one needs our attention
This one's wounds will keep
That one's leg is shattered
That one's chest is raw
That one just won't make it
But that's not the last I saw
Morning turns to evening
And still they bring boys in
There's no rest for the weary
And the night begins again

Landstuhl Hospital

(Operation Iraqi Freedom)
Dario R. Beniquez

Khalid is that you? Khalid Safi is that you?
In the landscape of dreamland, a voice calls Khalid.
He's nowhere found. Perhaps, he went back to Baghdad,

or sitting, right now, in a café in Istanbul sipping a cup
of Turkish coffee. He is not here. He is not at Landstuhl
Hospital. I am not him, I tell the medical technician

who won't take no for an answer. I am here in Germany,
eyes closed, curled up in a waiting room, waiting for Doctor
Cariño to see me. But, all I see is the Texas landscape.

I see my apartment. I see *El Paseo del Rio*. I am not he,
Khalid, the unknown one, the missing one. Camp Sarafovo
took its toll. I wait for the technician to call me,

to get my name right, to see Doctor Cariño, to get better,
to join the others back in Camp Sarafovo to end
this God forsaken war.

Mud - Army 116th Field Hospital
Mike Dailey

Mud
Everyday it rains – and then there's mud
Clean room?
    No way, in the mud and the humidity and the heat
    Under a green canvas tent
    In a clearing in a tropical jungle
The same thing every day, every week, every month
Triage the incoming
    Fix those that can be fixed
    Bag those that can't
    Relieve the pain and suffering of those that survive
    On a cot, in the heat, the humidity
    Surrounded by mud in a clearing of a tropical jungle
Until
    You send the invalids back to the states
    Ship the bags of the dead with them
    Send the wounded/repaired back to their units
    With the possibility of return
To
    The green canvas tents in the clearing
    Of a tropical jungle
    Where it rains every day
    And then – there is
Mud

IN MEMORIAM

No Way to Die

Dario R. Beniquez

I bury my toy soldiers,
for once and for all,
in the backyard.
Every Saturday,
I check on them.
I want to make
sure, they are safe
in their tiny coffins.
I want them
to stay there.
Yet when I think
of the number
of Armenians killed,
the killing fields where
bodies reside,
El Holocausto,
and the millions
yet to come,
they rise, rise,
the buried soldiers.
They inhabit flesh,
join the machinations
of tactical minds.
Then I think,
we may all vanish
in the shine of an eye
by a mere thumb's up.
There is no way
to bury the dead.

An Epitaph
decades after World War II & the US Army-Air Corps
William Conelly

It seems a garden name 'writ small'
—in twilight barely writ at all—
although he toiled his little days,
earned modicums of wage and praise,
financed a home, kept child and wife—

deprived no other man of life.
Or so we thought when growing up,
in lands beyond the bombers' drone,
the cities blown to dust and bone,
the powdered cultures snowing *up*.

What's his name now? A seed to sow
on blasted landscapes we shan't know?
A spider's line cast from the dead
so readers catch a sticky thread
and contemplate *their* little lives?

A swallow tips the wind and dives
for insects on the temperate air.
How like an ardent bird he flew
the horrid gusts that wartime blew—
and kept the ruin his affair.

November 11, 2018

(After Lyric in Time of War, American String Quartet, Veterans Day)
Dario R. Beniquez

The dead speak. They talk to us in dreams,
tell us what we do not see,
what we see, on the TV screen.

Suffer not falling bombs

Suffer not dismemberment

Love thy Neighbor as Thyself

How shall we void the clouds of destruction?
How shall we void the army of explosives?

Can our ears heed a human cry?

The dead do not lie. They come back
like somber knights of the dead

to take our flesh, to remind us we are a step away
from the army of the dead,

or time us on their ghostly watches to see
how long it will take us to rise again.

Memorial Day 2015
Janet Fagal

The last trumpet student my 85-year-old father had, asked him to be his mentor for his Eagle Scout project, Bugles Across America. At my father's funeral, on a very cold late October day on Long Island, NY, his student asked to play a final Taps for my dad, who had played Taps at every Veteran's Day, Memorial Day and 4th of July ceremony in our town and others on Long Island continuously since 1945. An Army Air Corps Base bugler at Randolph Field, San Antonio, during WWII, my father honored all who served. He would have been here today playing again, if he were still alive. I hear his amazing horn, so similar to his hero, Louis Armstrong, playing Taps, either solo or as the echo. Remembering and honoring. And thanking. Memorial Day is for all of us, but it is so much for you, too, Dad. I thank you. And thank you to his student, Georgie, who played Taps for him, and his other protege, Bob, who took this photograph for us to treasure. My father chose this final resting place for him and his family. If you look closely you can see that the sun came out from the rain at this precise time. There are shadows on the ground. Amazing. Grace.

In memoriam for you, Dad, Felix Sangenito.
July 9, 1920 – Oct. 21, 2005.

Elegy Over-due

Rachael Ikins

That woman sharp-shooter
we talked about the other night?
Let's bring her up again.
The one who shot so many of our men?
Inevitably they imported a rifle-master
from the 69th infantry and he took
care of her.

I saw her fall. The next morning, we returned.
Still she lay crumpled by a deadfall tree.
Autumn. No jacket. 45 year old
woman, feminine face, reddish hair streaking toward gray,
plain uniform skirt rucked around her knees, German skirt
same khaki worn by American WACS.
I was one of those who touched
her body.

We searched her in the stillness of cool forest—
No necklace, no rings nor bracelet, not dog-tags, no wallet.
Nameless.
Her shirt had bars on the lapel but no rank. There she lay,
crumpled, left-behind we were
stunned. How they could abandon this hero as if she were just
used equipment, thrown away, exhausted of purpose, landscape litter.

I worried for years about notifying her family. Her mother.
She looked old enough to be my own mom. I thought of those relatives
clustered like hands in prayer or fists around a radio. Listening.
Waiting for a knock on a door.
Someone said, "I think she was on a suicide mission."
Yeah, makes sense. I bet the Nazis forced her to join up.
Maybe she was a farm wife good with a gun, conscripted or
a Jewish woman who thought if she did what they asked
her children would go free.

We organized a burial detail, gave her a decent service.
What a shot this woman was, what an eye she had.
Sounds insane, I know. You had to be there.

I am 81 now. Some full-moon nights
she appears in my dreams. Just as I last saw her.
She opens her mouth to tell me
her name,

then everything will be alright. Never is.
She lies still in an autumn field somewhere
in Germany,
unknown soldier.

Sunlit Stone
Maureen Teresa McCarthy

The wall marches long
Rising and falling
Under the cruel bright sun
Lighting the world
They did not live to see

Here are the young men
Who have never grown old
Under the cool silver moon
Restless and wild no more

Names – etched in granite
Row after row after row
Names
On polished stone
All that remains
Of laughter living loving
Their names
In memory

We who are left
Stand in the warm sun
With the flowers and the medals
Tokens from a harsh prison
Forgotten history.

Shotwell Memorial Park
Judith McGinn

swathe of green beside a lake
where the town band plays on summer nights
children pinwheel beneath leafy elms
on Veterans Day squadrons of flags march across the sky
Shotwell Memorial Park stands watch at western end
strong shoulders for a tender cheek

we often ambled there to read the plaques
with your hand you touched the past
traced names of family from this hometown
Spanish American War your ancestor served
with grit and hope your grandpa survived
the war that failed to end them all
your Dad sprinted through WW II in administration
your name leaps out under Vietnam
a catch in my throat, unwanted tears
on the Mekong River you commanded boats
heat and war were savage
on patrol one afternoon
snipers' bullets ripped from shore
splintered wood and blood, a man was killed
you didn't speak of it for years until
in Washington you traced his name
on the wall like a wound in the ground and you,
your eyes blurred with tears remembering

after tours patrolling the Persian Gulf
in another ongoing war
our son oceans away near Tokyo
back here at home in Shotwell Park
his name is added to the rest
on a new curved wall like open arms
he faces fountain, flag and you
I traced his name today

AFTERMATH

Unattached

Fee Thomas

My mother, in tears, used to come home and respectfully tell us about them. Grown men. Crying out. Writhing in pain. Vietnam Vets. Apathetic, unknowledgeable doctors couldn't make sense of it. For the thing they were screaming about - their limb - was vanished in a jungle. Somewhere. No longer attached. Why did it hurt so bad? We buried him on the first of the month. Lowered him to the ground. Gave him to nature, to God. But still, I cry out. I writhe. It makes no sense. My sibling no longer attached. Lost in an instant. Pain demanding to be felt just the same.

Thanks, Belated

J.G. in the AFA English Department
William Conelly

Major, I owe you what
anyone might owe a stranger
met in lamplight down
a charcoal maze of streets:

the thanks for good directions
patiently dispensed where
anyone might stand convinced
I had been vaguely sent.

But more, I owe you for
this life long afterwards:
hallways and rooms beyond
a secret seeming door.

Gipper Hugh and the Train
Pat Hardigree

My family called me TJ ever since I could remember. My given names are Thomas James. I started the 8th grade at the McElroy Junior High school in Trenton, a new kid on the block. A group of guys started bullying me after school. I didn't like to fight, and I didn't know how to handle those that did. I simply stopped going to school. My mother arranged for me to go and live with my sister, Rose, and her husband, Gipper and their four kids in Bend, Oregon for a few months. Mom sent money to them for my board. I liked it there and I liked the school in Bend. The kids were different than the ones I knew in New Jersey. Nicer, I think. I got along with them but had no real friends yet. Gipper gave me a list of chores to do the first day I was there. He told me we all work in this house. When he came home from work, he asked me first thing if I did my assignments. I learned to do my chores as soon as I got home from school, and then my homework.

He teased me about leaving New Jersey and my Mom. "Wait until you meet some of those big mean boys here. They'll have you up for lunch. I'll show you how to stand up to bullies. Doesn't matter how big or small you are. It's attitude, boy. Pure attitude."

Gipper was a Vietnam Veteran and he had been wounded there. He told me he had a steel plate in his head, and he had to take medication to prevent seizures. He was irritable a lot, but sometimes he'd talk to me like I was a grownup. Gipper taught Auto Shop and history at the local high school. He knew a lot about everything and liked to explain things to me.

After we finished dinner on Friday night that week, he said that we were going for a hike tomorrow, it being a Saturday. He usually had some work to do on the house, or we would all get into his old jeep and go somewhere. He looked at me. "Be ready. I want to introduce you to the Oregon Wilderness." He got up and went to bed, which meant he had one of his "malignant headaches." That's what he called them. He had medicine that made him sleep and my sister Rose and her four kids and myself, had better be tiptoeing around the house. No noise was the rule. We didn't want him to get up and start throwing things around breaking them.

He was up early and shook me out of sleep. "We're leaving."

I jumped into my clothes and put on a pair of Gipper's old shoes Rose found for me. They almost fit with two pairs of socks. She made me wear one of his old vests as the weather was turning cold, and a skull cap. She gave me some granola cookies she made and her water canteen for my backpack. I noticed Gipper wasn't wearing a pack, and he was drinking down a bottle of water. We picked up Coates, a fellow teacher that taught math, and something else I didn't get. He wore a backpack and he and Gipper both wore hiking boots. Gipper called his dog, Bones, a black Labrador mix. "He needs to get used to the woods. I'll take him hunting with me when I go. You, too."

Gipper parked his Jeep in an area park south of Bend. We hiked for a couple of hours from there through forested land and came across the railroad tracks. Gipper told me that we were going to walk the tracks since we were going through a lava flow and the ground was rocky and rough. He explained that the lava flow came from active volcanos thousands of years ago. The train needed to go through, so a roadway about twelve feet across was cleared for the tracks for many miles. The Lava flow was as much as thirty feet deep in some places and walls were put up on both sides to hold it back.

We stopped for a bit to take it all in. I took the cookies sharing them with Gipper and Coates, who had brought sandwiches and two small cartons of milk. Coates didn't know I was coming and had not brought extra food. Gipper handed me half of one of his sandwiches. "Got to be prepared, boy. Better learn that. Mom isn't here to make your lunch." He gave Bones some treats, and Coates poured a bit of his water into one of the cartons he opened with a knife for the dog.

I drank my water. I was so thirsty I finished all of it. They were careful that none of their garbage was left. I put the bag that held the cookies into my backpack, glad I hadn't discarded it and hear a lecture from Gipper.

We came across a dead deer and a coyote on the tracks. Gipper said it looked like the deer was hit by a train, and then the coyote feeding on it got hit by another one. The train comes through so fast, if you see it coming and you're on the tracks, you can't get off fast enough, so we must listen for the train. Gipper showed me how to listen by putting his ear on the rail. He told me he had a schedule and knew about when the trains were running. The dog stayed on the tracks sometimes sprinting ahead so that Gipper had to call him back.

We walked the tracks through the lava flow that became so high walls had been built up. Gipper said we would stand pressing ourselves against the wall as the train was passing through. I saw him and Coates checking the rail every so often listening for the train. "Not long now. It must be coming through Bend." He checked his watch and listened to the rail. "It's coming now. Get off the track."

Coates pressed himself against the wall and yelled at me to get off the track. I looked at Gipper who was down some ways ahead of us calling his dog who just stood in the middle of the track. Coates moved to where I was and pulled me roughly by the shirt to the wall. "Stay here. I don't feel like scraping you up." I stayed and tried to call the dog off the tracks as Gipper was calling too. The dog seemed uncertain where to go and just stood there looking from side-to-side until he saw the train and tried to run away on the tracks, but the train was coming fast and almost in front of us the dog was hit.

I dared not move as the train was passing by. It was only inches away from me and time seemed to last long minutes, and it was gone. Gipper was running on the track looking for Bones. The body had been thrown against the wall, crumpled and bloodied. I stayed with Coates who admonished me that I should have kept my mouth shut. We joined Gipper kneeling, staring at his dog. I looked at its open eyes. Gipper told me to give him my backpack and the old vest I was wearing. He took them and made a contraption to wrap the dog's body so that it could be carried. He hung the dog on me balancing the weight from my arms and shoulders. "You carry him. When it becomes too much, I'll take him."

I nodded and started walking. We turned back on the tracks and I figured it would be three or more hours before we reached the car.

Gipper, TJ and Bones
Pat Hardigree

The scalp over the steel plate in my head
pounded like bombs going off, like the train passing
in front of TJ and me yesterday. I got up to relieve myself

picked up my bottle of meds and went into the kitchen.
The nightlight was on. I poured water into a glass,
got ice out, reached back into the cabinet for the gin

and poured out a healthy amount and drank it down.
My young brother-in-law, TJ, stood in the hallway.
Gipper gestured. *You want one? I won't tell your Mom.*

Yeah, he said. I filled his glass and poured in a splash of gin.
TJ took the glass. *Are you going to bury Bones?*
I'll dig the grave. Where do you want it?

I poured another glass and downed it with my meds.
There's a spot on the back side of the house.
He was a good dog. Kids loved him.

TJ blurted out, *I wanted to get Bones off the track*
but I was too scared. I'm sorry. It's my fault.
Gipper told him it was an accident. *Stuff happens.*

TJ downed his drink. *I felt like I was going to fall*
under the wheels and be killed. And afterwards
I was thinking, Bones is gone but I'm still here.

You looked at me like you wanted to kill me.
I thought you might beat me up, but you made me
carry Bones back. I was never so thirsty in my life.

Yeah, Gipper said. *I'll mark out the grave before I leave.*
Three feet deep. 3 by 4 is good. Square off the corners.
You're a man now boy. You can handle it.

Return From Vietnam
Pat Hardigree

Gipper Hugh Grimes, Vietnam Vet, 1949-1994

They put our heads on stakes.
We learned from our mistakes.

Ho Chi Minh sent them in
to kill us all, and we killed them.

Bloody rage, bloody days,
blood and flesh, a bloody haze.

They gave us all a new belief.
Pounded us without relief.

"They're not human. They're gooks."
They come at night like spooks.

Kill them or be killed.
You have the guns and the skills.

And we killed and killed and they killed us.
In the day we died, at night we cursed

and killed and killed and killed again
and they killed us. There seemed no end.

Our reward: a three-day pass.
We went to Saigon and had a blast.

I came back home to greet the snow.
I tried to live and just let go.

We killed those of another race.
But they wore boots and had a face.

Whole families were set afire.
It's the truth. I'm not a liar.

They were human. Oh, humanity!
I can't live with the thorns of banality.

Through the terror of my dreams I see
only one path appear to me.

Forgive me. No one else is to blame.
I'll walk the tracks into the train.

I have the skill to kill.
God help me. I have the will.

Austere Airfield

(Southwest Asia)
Dario R. Beniquez

"Who can I kill?" the sign read.
I thought it read, "Who can I heal?"

So I walked around with my hand
outstretched like a holy man,

attempting to heal the lame, blind,
and despondent—to no effect. But

I did not come here to heal,
but to search for a launching pad to hush

the incurable, the politically skewed,
to set them down on the righteous path

to democratic ends.

Dog Tags in Hand
Angela Sobery

The humility of society dangles beneath a rugged
and worn blistered hand.
This hand has touched lives all over the world, but that fist has
been determined to protect his family first.
These military tags drape down the fist projecting the honor of
tradition and civic duty that defines America's legacy.
The single red metallic dog tag classifies
his human vulnerability of ailing deficiencies.
However, the grey tarnished tags impose
an endless remembrance of a hero that bestowed chivalry.
These metallic tokens of exhilarating honor
are not only worn to identify a worthy soul, but to define the
greatness of humanity.

Labor Day
Dwain Wilder

I have seen the American folk taken as a cruel harvest
Seen them mowed from their roots and craft
Seen them bagged like leaves, like shredded secrets,
    collected on the empty fields of their own homes,
    bulldozed by mortgages and Urban Renewal into
    landfills
    and capped daily with an impervious clay of official
    policy.

I have seen them in the fish markets of Capitalism and
    Globalism,
    trying to flip back into the ocean of their labor —
    now far away —
    craftspeople, secretaries, engineers, farmers,
    factory workers, aircraft fabricators, software programmers,
    suddenly sent slithering into the holding pens of un
    necessary prey,
    their jobs obliterated or taken overseas to those glad   for
the dimes.
    Seen them pacing streets, left with pocket change,
    begging at intersections to work for food,
    given programs run from surplus desks in abandoned
    buildings by begrudging bureaucrats.
    Seen their energy distracted, their contrariness
    broken,
    their native work hobbled, their creativity managed to
    death.
Seen the knowing nods and companionable sympathy
    from war veterans and welfare moms —
    been there, still doing that, crazy with it.

I have seen the American folk like plains of wheat,
    gathered from over the earth
    enriching the vision and courage of the land.
Seen them scythed in a fell salvation
    by preachers called, they say, by Jesus
    to the seat of American power from now til
    Armageddon,
    the obedient to be swept up in Rapture,
    knowers of Truth,

baiters of men, women, blacks,
    baiters of muslims, jews, trade unionists,
    baiters of lesbos, queers and other wildlife,
    dividing & twisting,
    dividing & twisting,
    until one skein doesn't know
    its sisters and brothers the next skein over,
    though shoulder to shoulder they be.

I have seen them derided for not giving their daughters and
    sons to war, while the evangelists of American empire
    quietly hide their own,
Seen their children answer the call of duty
    or dodge the draft
    or get drafted
    sent to hold the checkpoints of American hegemony,
    battling for everything back home
    against people standing in their own homes.
Seen them come back alone, unblessed,
    mangled, sometimes mocked,
    spat on by pacifists,
    covered in the ironic excrement of war's glory.

Seen them insulted for knowing that, for paying too much
    attention
    for not paying enough attention
    for not shopping, for owing too much
    for being fat, for being scrawny.
Seen them insulted for having sex and children and poverty
    and sorrow
    instead of loneliness — then having the loneliness after
    all
    for having sex when you don't want babies
    for needing an abortion even though you abhor
    abortions.
Seen them insulted for living too long, for not being old
    enough
    for voting while black, while poor,
    for being too black, not black enough.
Seen them insulted for being too smart, too dumb,
    too lost, too saved,
    too punked out, too goth,
    profiled likely to be packing heat at school.

I have seen the American folk chumped by admen, salesmen,
    pitchmen, spammers,
    public relations hucksters,
    cooing celebs certain you want
    to buy their lipstick,
    growled at to buy pickup trucks or luxury behemoths
    or combat vehicles
    to drive under the sparkling sun through
    your maple-shady
    life of ease.
Buy yer drugs, getcher doc to prescribe 'em (or not).
Buy stocks, buy bonds, buy a gun — two, three —
    Belligerence Is Your American Right.
Drink beer lotsa beer, drink pepsi, drink coke,
    drink cranapple —
    drink *something* for chrissakes.
Shave your face, shave your legs, shave your ass,
    wax your crotch.
Buy pretty perfume
    buy your dreams
    buy your life.
Be sexy.
Be powerful with remote control
    in the blue glamour of your TV.

I have seen us fist-fighting in street clothes on Jerry Springer.
Seen us dying of news poisoning,
    wan faces considering the phony voices
    blasting out of the televisions bolted to the ceiling.
Seen us drowning in the blood of innocents we have bombed
    all the way into Jeffersonian Democracy
    then all the way back out again.
Seen us drowning in the CIA's assassinations.
Seen us swamped by our own butlers of terror day after day
with no end
    at the School of the Americas
    at Gitmo at Abu Graib at Bagram
    at black prisons who knows where.
Seen us choked with the effort to speak
    what our bones know
    as we hang by our tongues from America.

We cry out for one!
We cry out for one who will convene the American folk

Away from dreams of empire
Away from wars of adventure
Away from foreign policy made of explosions, poisons and fear.

We cry out for one who will convene the American folk
To belong to the American land.
We are its forests
We are its rivers
We are its cities and towns, the scintillating life of its streets
We, the lakes on its breast
We, the long marches of its prairie
We are the obdurate activity of its mountains, the black obsidian
of their deep fire.
We are its heart, its mind.
Our thoughts, our dreams,
Our hopes for our kin and our folk, for our nation, for its soil
Are none other than this American continent,
Its aspirations, its long meditation.
Our lives are the tides of its dream.

Sunrise Service
William Conelly

Cathedral windows—stained
with cobalt, manganese,
rose gold, oxides of tin—
declare an arch intent
to colour our designs,
sacred or saccharin.

> *Potential is the thought—*
> *or simple wish—for doing*
> *all that waits undone,*
> *the gain of it aside,*
> *the loss of it the same*
> *for sage or simpleton.*

The choir sweetly sings.
Dawn's angels rise anew.
Our sense of sound exceeds
our congregated thought,
and from its resonance
—again—darkness recedes.

Surprising Benediction
Janet Fagal

We always heard the story,
how he rode the train
for four of his five
days of leave.
 All the way
from San Antonio
to New York
and back.
It was World War II
and he wanted to see her.
For even one day.
The train. Changed so much
of history. Rails bringing
the circus or the camper,
the worker or the friend.
Connected by the hum
of the wheels.
 Tasting time
in quick breaths
 between stations,
the train
as certain as the heart.
Riders tucked in a berth
 or a seat,
on a bench or alone.
How much do so many owe
 to a train,
trailing puffs of steam,
screeching toward home?

The Soldier
Rachael Ikins

He came home in '68.
2005 I met him
in the chiropractor's
waiting room. A handsome
man, fifty-ish, well-dressed,
a gold chain, flat links
around his neck.
We spoke of unintentional ice-
dancing, falls, and
the virtue of walking home
from a beer party, how
even church parking lots can
be unsafe.

We spoke of war.
I had worn a bracelet with
A missing pilot's name,
this man, a machine gun.

Defoliant had killed all the trees
where he was stationed, the mud,
the Viet Cong bullet that sliced
through his life with chaotic precisions.

How he lay face-down
in that mud his red blood
leaking, leaking into thirsty
Earth, how cold it is in the jungle
after all.

We talked of gardens
to plant soon and
healing green.

His eyes flicker like wild horses running
his childhood torn in pieces strewn
across tropical forest loam,
another life *and death* ago.
Gary. His name
is Gary.

War Is Not Just War
~After Walt Whitman's As I Ponder'd in Silence
Laurie Kolp

I hear this Phantom calling out to you
as you ponder in silence, linger long
and consider the essence of your poems.
This Phantom, whose menacing voice
points fingers to immortal songs,
has the genius of poets half-correct—
war IS a common theme for bards across time,
but let's put things in perspective here
so that this Phantom voice might understand.
This is where I agree with you, Walt
about the battles of life and death
on fields of the world, a weight on our shoulders
like the backpacks soldiers must carry
for miles and miles through wind and rain
jungles, marshes, across oceans.
Our problems encountered at various times—
conflict, disquietude, unease
life and death, body and soul—
we hold on our backs through the trenches
of years spent on earth braving
demons that try and cause suffering.
And like Shakespeare said,
(although this is thought for another poem)
"All the world's a stage, and we are merely players."
Players are people
are soldiers
is war
is the world
is us.
War is not just war.

The Purple-hearted Hero
Rachael Ikins

you and I lie
in the dark and hold hands like
two children facing the edge of the forest
Wilderness and we go down to the trenches.

where a best friend died and sheltered you
with his body until
the Germans with their stabbing bayonets left.
where a woman became a sniper
for reasons unknown *why would anyone*
want to do that and she shot your friends
one by one
right between the eyes
until

one day someone killed her
one clean blow.
I imagine she died as she wished,
a peculiar sort of hero.

we look at the time
you tracked
another enemy soldier
who was picking off your men,
when everybody crawled everywhere for to raise
you head was instant death. you followed him,
on your belly, with your knife,

both of you 18 years old and sons of mothers
who prayed far away. He smiled as he died
when you slit his throat and your buddies slapped
your back and called you "hero."

you have spent just about forever
wishing you could take that moment of slash-and-fire
back. you returned state-side and became a doctor.

we whisper of these things
in our cloud of darkness
and fight our private wars with the demons
who steal sleep.

for in the seething night
don't all memories wander home,
hanging out drunk and smelling of weed
on the porch, jostling,
begging for you to wash their dirty clothes

at just the moment when you
most wish it is safe
to turn your back.

The Scars of War
Bernie Conklin

A picture on a mantel of a loved one lost at sea.
Dreams of a life together that will never, ever be.

Searing scars on a mom's heart who learns she has lost a son,
when presented with the flag; tribute for a job well done.

A young wife and mother too; a somber knock on her door;
two men dressed in uniforms; she collapses on the floor.

The plight of untold children whose dads they will never see.
Millions go into battle; to survive, their humble plea.

Scenes so bad, so horrific they're locked up in the mind.
This type of villainous scar may be the most heinous kind.

Countless thousands missing limbs with entire futures to live.
Heroes all, they go to fight; sworn even their lives to give.

The damage to property is possible to repair,
yet scars on humanity are absolute; always there.

We have even fought ourselves because we could not agree;
a terrible civil war, instead of diplomacy.

War has always been a part of the things that people do.
Why that is I do not know. Sad it is, but all too true.

After any contention pardon is a must.
But, can it be possible to ever restore the trust?

No amount of forgiveness; no expressions of regret;
can erase the scars of war; those, we never can forget.

The Bond ©2019 Ben Appplebaum

I have spent 8 years as an Active Duty US Army photographer, and am currently continuing my service in the Army Reserve. My assignments have ranged from the White House, US Army Special Operations Command, and the Army Reserve's only Combat Camera unit. This image speaks to the bond that develops between Soldiers, regardless of age, race, sex, or preference, just by simply serving alongside each other. These bonds live on to span both time and distance.

~ Ben Applebaum

ONLY SOLDIERS KNOW

Lying the Truth
Mark Blickley

One of the happiest days of my life occurred during the winter of 1973. I was on military leave from the Air Force and it's an understatement to say that I needed much more than a three-week vacation. I was on the verge, or probably more accurately, in the midst of a nervous breakdown.

I'd pulled a tour of Vietnam. The past few months I had been finishing out my enlistment at Charleston Air Force Base in South Carolina. The war was a sour experience, but what deepened my depression and anxiety was the peacetime service. After the fear and excitement and brotherhood of combat, I was deposited on a base full of non-combatants pretending to be hard-ass military men.

I had blocked in aircraft half-naked on the flight line while enemy rockets fell around me. At Charleston AFB if a button wasn't mated with a hole or a boot lacked a glossy polish, or God forbid, a hair was touching my ear, I'd be jumped on like I'd just set fire to the American flag. Instead of support and relief, we Vets received hostility and harassment for our lack of military bearing. Glowing write-ups while under fire met nothing; a real man didn't replace his government issue boxer shorts with Fruit of the Loom jockey briefs.

My unhappiness ripened into confusion and envy.

Everyone else seemed to be adjusted or adjusting. Everyone else seemed to be happy. My sadness frightened me. I felt as if I was shut out of some universal secret. I truly believed that there was some kind of personal information that hadn't been passed on to me. Even the drugs I was consuming at the time were not agents of euphoria. Instead of offering a numbing comfort they simply increased my awareness of how alienated and needy I had become.

My behavior had become so erratic that my First Sergeant "strongly suggested" I take an immediate leave and straighten myself up. My last words to him before I left his office were the same words I was asking everyone I met, stranger or acquaintance.

"Are you happy?" I asked.

My First Sergeant eyed me with suspicion. I was totally sincere. "Yeah, I'm happy," he muttered.

"Why? Can you tell me why?" I pleaded.

He cleared his throat and said, "Because I'm getting rid of your ass for a few weeks, that's why I'm happy." He was being totally sincere too.

Now this may seem a bit silly or naive, but I felt like the only way I could pull myself out of this debilitating funk was to try and understand how and why others could be so functional and contented. My opening question, "are you happy?" was always, and I mean always answered in the affirmative.

The sources of all this happiness were quite varied. It could be a girlfriend, a job, a car, a good bottle of cognac, anything. The point is that no one told me they were unhappy. No one. My question didn't give me any answers I could use as clues. It just made feel more depressed and estranged.

During the course of my three week leave I visited my older sister who was working her way through college as a belly dancer. She was living somewhere Upstate New York, Jamestown, I think. I met her at the club she was working and was given the keys to her apartment. She told me to just relax there until her performance ended; I'd be seeing her in a few hours.

I remember being stretched out on her living room floor, smoking a joint, listening to an eight track of Emerson, Lake and Palmer's Pictures at an Exhibition when I heard a knock on the door. I opened the door on a small, incredibly stacked young woman with a southern accent. I introduced myself to my sister's neighbor. This sexy young woman, Becky, invited me to wait over at her apartment. I eagerly accepted. I could tell by her friendly and aggressive behavior that she was attracted to me. As I pulled my sister's door shut behind me I could already feel my face smothered inside Becky's perfumed cleavage.

I wasn't feeling too thrilled with life; I took comfort wherever I could find it.

My hormonal heat flared as we entered her one room apartment. We sat on the couch facing the biggest framed photograph I'd ever seen.

Actually it wasn't a photo at all. It was a poster of a sleazy looking man of late middle age. This skinny poster boy had sparse, greased back hair and a kind of moustache popular in the thirties a thin pencil line of facial hair underlining his large nose. Beneath his grinning portrait, in bold letters, I read FRANK COLE, A&P MANAGER OF THE MONTH. The month was August, 1971. I admired Frank's courage in exposing his dental work. Even though the photo was in black and white you could tell his teeth had to be green.

The ornately framed poster dominated the tiny room. I fought back my laughter. I didn't want to insult Becky's father. I just wanted to bang his daughter.

Well, Becky talked and talked and talked. What I mistook for her lust seemed to be a genuine affection for my sister that she transferred to me. As soon as I realized this I shifted from horny G.I. to soul-searching outcast.

"Are you happy?" I asked Becky.

Becky beamed and nodded.

"Why?"

Becky pointed to the Manager of the Month. "It's because of Frankie. He's the most wonderful man in the world."

I glanced over at the poster and it made me sick to think of that guy with this lovely, sweet girl. Becky was definitely on the sunny side of twenty-five.

She launched into a description of Frankie Cole that was so loving and awe-inspired, by the time she finished her tribute to him his portrait started looking handsome to me too.

When my sister arrived I gave Becky a goodnight peck on the cheek. I was more depressed than ever. It's not that I be-grudged Becky her joy, but even a guy like Frankie Cole was able to attain a state of happiness. And here I was, a twenty year old in wonderful shape with a full head of hair and nice set of teeth, feeling like the most miserable man on earth.

The first words my sister said to me after we entered her apartment was that she hoped I hadn't taken advantage of Becky because she was a really good person.

Take advantage? What was she talking about? How could I take advantage of Becky? I never met anyone who was as much in love as was Becky. Who could possible hope to compete with August 1971's A&P Manager of the Month, Frankie Cole?

My sister shook her head. She told me that Becky had engaged in an affair with Frank Cole a couple of years ago when he was manager of the Produce department and she was a part-time grocery clerk. Frank was married and told the teenage Becky how horrible his wife was and how miserable his life had become. Frank arranged to have Becky transferred to Produce and they shared passion for about a year amongst the fruit and vegetation. During this time Frank would pacify Becky by promising to divorce his wife.

Becky, feeling so sorry for her man, called Frank's wife and demanded she set Frankie free from his house of torture. The next day Frank had Becky transferred out of Produce. He tried to end their relationship but Becky wouldn't listen. She was a woman in love. After Becky began making weekly calls to Frank's wife, he had Becky transferred out of his store and into an A&P some sixty miles away. He refused to see her.

My sister informed me that Becky's life now consisted entirely of working at the new A&P five days a week. On Becky's two days off she'd drive over to her former supermarket and sit in her parked car for hours, watching her beloved through the store's large windows. Frankie Cole had abandoned her, wouldn't even look at her, but Becky would not and could not abandon the man she loved.

My response to my sister's version of Becky's story was anger. Becky had lied to me! I was vulnerable and she lied to me! I had asked for help and she teased me with her broken fantasies of emotional well-being.

That night the three of us went out to dinner at a local diner. My hostility towards Becky manifested itself by my total silence during the heavy, grease-laden meal. I observed her like a scientist waiting for a disastrous reaction in his laboratory. Frank Cole's name was never brought up. Becky was charming. And warm. And sweet. And funny. My anger melted into pity. By the time dessert arrived I had had a catharsis, along with a touch of gas.

I realized that Becky and all the others I questioned hadn't lied to me. Claiming they were happy and giving me their reasons for their happiness was an act of kindness and hope. I knew that Becky's love crisis was every bit as intense as my military crisis, yet she was a model of grace under pressure. Her imagination had provided her with the ability to still experience pleasure despite the awesome burden of a crushing reality.

If fantasy was allowing her to function at such a high level, well, I thought, God bless the human imagination and its ability to construct protective worlds of security and satisfaction. That was the secret I was searching for. Like Becky, I had found it inside Frankie Cole's imposing icon.

Although the food from that diner dinner repeated itself throughout the night and into the early morning, it was the best meal I ever consumed. I learned to swallow my self-pity watching Becky that night.

Troglodyte
Michael Brady

I have been fierce
        in judgment.
I have burned
        in anger.
I have been blinded by poisons—
        and self.

Now, a wren:
        shelter,
        sustenance,
        a song to sing.

Door Gunner

(John Zavala of Rockaway)
Dario R. Beniquez

I am not surprised if there
is a bullet with my DNA
etched on it.

Now, I walk twisted
as everyone sees.

My life's a shopping cart
things go in, things go out.

I am a soldier inside my grief.
Who says things will get better?

The monsoon hits hard. Helicopter
down, 600 rounds—if you please.

Babas
Sandra Flores-Surprise

What makes *babas**
spontaneously smile
their openhearted, gap-toothed grins,
that endearingly crinkle the skin
at the corners of their kind, dancing eyes,
at the sight of you?

Babas that are being cared for
by the children of their children:
their sons and daughters
who were slaughtered and discarded
in shallow unmarked graves.

What compels *babas*
to eagerly reach out and take your hand
or to affectionately embrace you
as only a grandmother can?

You, in your BDUs**, and Kevlar helmet,
and flak vest, and battle rattle***.
You, with your military issued M16 rifle
slung over your shoulder;
a weapon designed for the sole purpose
to kill too.

*grandma
**Battle Dress Uniform
***full combat gear worn by a soldier

Gerszewski Barracks

(78th Engineer Battalion)
Dario R. Beniquez

Pass the bowl, not the rice bowl,

but the bowl stashed with hash,

black Afghanistan, the good stuff,

said a frizzy hair soldier from Dallas,

as soldiers jostled each other,

played Spades, listened to Santana's

Hope You're Feeling Better,

laughed out loud, getting high

as endorphins kicked-in sending

them spinning to the funhouse,

while *actually* smoking camel crap.

The Soldier ©2019 Ben Applebaum

This image serves as a reminder that each and every Soldier is a person, with their own history, family, and feelings. Many times, military members are lumped together as a large group. It is easy to forget that each Soldier, Sailor, Airman, Marine, and Coast Guardsman is a unique person with their own unique story.

~Ben Applebaum

Tour of Duty
Whit Schweizer

I. Sharp Rocks

When I awakened my stomach was clenched into hard ripples that lay over a sinking-into-an abyss feeling. I had been running in slow motion, trying as hard as I could to run faster, but unable to stay ahead of the huge orange street sweeper. The machine growled and roared. A half-dozen or so screaming gremlin-like beings rode on its outer surface, the way soldiers ride on tanks. With great effort, like running at "play time" in the YMCA pool where I was learning to swim, I could slow down the great machine's rate of approach. But the sucking sound coming from the black hole between the spinning brushes continued to come closer and closer until I was about to be swept under and inhaled into the street sweeper's belly. I woke up just before the whirling brushes caught me. I crawled into bed with my mother to seek comfort.

The nightmare recurred until my father returned from Korea. His first night home I had the nightmare five or six times, and each time sought comfort by crawling into their bed. He sent me away to my own room gently at first, then more and more loudly and firmly. Eventually he took me by the arm, guided me back to my room and thrust me onto my bed. He told me, "Stay there or there will be consequences." Going to my mother's bed to seek comfort had been O.K, in fact welcomed, for over two years. A parent that I barely remembered had returned after being gone for what seemed like most of my life and completely changed the rules. The injustice of it all overwhelmed me with rage. I sobbed unconsolably.

The drive to be comforted goaded me back to their room. My father leapt out of bed and grabbed me just before I made it to my refuge. As he carried me under one arm, he said he was going to teach me to "be considerate of others." On the way back to my room he picked up a long-handled hairbrush with his free hand. He tossed me onto my bed, pulled down my pajama pants and voiced the parental apology of the fifties. "It hurts me more to do this than it hurts you." He spanked my bare bottom with the shoehorn end of the hairbrush until it felt stinging hot. I couldn't believe that the spanking hurt him more than it hurt me.

As I sat painfully on the edge of my bed I made a decision to become "perfect," which meant perfectly obedient, so I would never again feel such agony. I decided that I could measure my progress toward perfection by what others thought of me, especially my father.

Until my teens I had little relationship with my father except as a disciplinarian. The discipline and order he practiced as a Navy Reserve Officer carried over to our home life. My sister, three years my senior, referred to him as "Cap'n Daddy Sir" when he was out of ear shot. I remember being something of a comedian before he came home from Korea. "Don't be a smart aleck," followed by the hairbrush in extreme cases, cured me of comedy. I focused on being "conscientious" and "considerate of others," traits that my father admired.

When I was eleven and old enough to join the Boy Scouts my relationship with my father broadened. Dad had been an Eagle Scout and was pleased when I wanted to join scouting. We both enjoyed the camping trips immensely. I enjoyed his relatively more relaxed stance toward discipline in the outdoors. His motto, "Always be considerate of others," took on an immediate, useful meaning. He taught me many techniques for conserving wilderness resources and to "always leave a campsite cleaner than you found it." I developed a new appreciation for the natural world, and independently of my father, a reverence for the sacred vitality that expresses itself best in nature.

Sharp rocks instruct me:
value the softness of grass;
tread lightly on earth.

Humble water flows,
sustains giant Sequoias,
pursues low places.

Balmy alpine sun
inflames unprotected skin,
dispels the morning mist.

My father told me,
"Catch only enough to eat.
Fish with self-tied flies."

Rainbows teach me myself:
Walk the creek unequipped;
eat biscuits and bacon for breakfast.

I eventually made Eagle Scout. Dad gave me the Eagle ribbon and medal he had earned three decades earlier. He had been neutral about the other achievements of my teenage years… straight "A"s in school, accomplishments as a clarinetist, President of the high school student body, but was pleased when I enlisted in the Navy at seventeen and earned a Navy scholarship to Stanford. When I graduated and was commissioned as an Ensign, Dad presented me with his officer's sword. I felt like I had been inducted into the manhood club.

II. Daughter on the Mountaintop

I saw Vietnam for the first time in 1971 during the first of two deployments to WESPAC, Navy speak for the Western Pacific war theater. I was totally unprepared for Vietnam's beauty. Images on television gave me the impression that Vietnam, except for Saigon, consisted of bombed-out, burned-out jungle. My impressions included women and children on fire, running from napalmed villages. Although these images may have been accurate in the interior, the reality of coastal Vietnam was quite different. The coast was unbelievably green. Miró could not have selected a more beautiful color. The verdant jungle lay beyond white strands of pristine beach and the turquoise clarity of shallow water near the coast. This was the view when we were stationed near the Demilitarized Zone, on the DMZ gun line. Our slate-grey ship firing its 5-inch cannons into all this beauty added to the war's surreality.

So did the scene of the fishermen as they exited the Cửa Việt River at the southern boundary of the DMZ. Every day just after sunup two dozen fishing boats came out of the mouth of the river to position themselves at a safe distance as we fired our cannons with great blasts of yellow-orange flame and blue-grey smoke. As bullets the size of footballs screamed over head the long narrow open boats, each filled with what looked like extended families… mothers, fathers, children, uncles, aunts, grandparents… fished all day, seemingly oblivious to our booming cannons. At dusk they returned to the small harbors that lined the Cửa Việt river. I envied the seeming simplicity of their lives and generational closeness. It reminded me of a simpler time when the US was a family centered agrarian society, and wary politicians warned of the folly of foreign wars. The display of the extended Vietnamese families also heightened my loneliness. I wondered why I was fighting this war thousands of miles from my family while the Vietnamese went about their daily lives.

Our orders on the gun line were to provide Naval gunfire in

support of the Marines interdicting North Vietnamese Army regulars crossing the DMZ. The Marine spotters would call in fire control coordinates on the encrypted radio. We would adjust our fire to hit the coordinates specified in the radio calls. For weeks the Marines had been complaining about the inaccuracy of naval gunfire. Despite my growing realization of the futility of the war, I decided to see if I could solve the problem of inaccurate gunfire. The "inner child" perfectionist who defers to authority took over. I thought, "I have to be here anyway, so I might as well excel at my job." I was going to do my best to kill NVA. First, I set my mind to observing the barrels of the five-inch guns to see if there was a reason that they aimed poorly. I noticed there was a slight judder in the barrels when the ship rolled, and the hydraulics tried to keep the guns steady on target. I had an idea that might increase the accuracy of our gunfire. I decided to try out my idea during my next watch as Officer of the Deck.

On my next watch I positioned the sea swells on the port bow to minimize the ship's rolling and watched bubbles on the water to monitor the ship's fore and aft motion. I issued as many engine orders as needed to keep the ship as still as possible. All stop… port ahead one third… starboard back one third… all back one third…. I issued order after order in rapid succession. I gave more than 350 engine orders during my four-hour watch, an average of one every 40 seconds. My deliberate, calculated measures to kill North Vietnamese soldiers worked. Rave reviews from the Marine spotters began to come across the encrypted radio. "Two trucks blown up… a platoon of NVA blown away… twenty-five more kills… no, fifty!" I was frequently rewarded with, "Good shooting!" from the voice on the radio. Toward the end of my watch a bright yellow spotter plane, a very powerful propeller driven plane known as a "Bronco" flew by at bridge level a few hundred yards off the starboard side, waggled its wings, gunned its engine and stood nearly on its tail as it ascended to about 5000 feet. A fellow junior officer came onto the bridge from the combat information center where he had been directing gunfire.

"Do you know what that was? That was an attaboy!" raved my buddy as he clapped me on my shoulders. "Not every ship gets one of those."

I reveled in the praise and wore the claps on my back like a cloak of glory… until the petty officer standing engineer of the watch came up to the bridge to have me sign the engine order log. Having the Officer of the Deck sign the "Bell Log" when ridiculous engine orders have been issued is a Navy tradition. It is about as much chastisement of an officer as an enlisted man is allowed. As

I signed the Bell Log the Captain came out on the bridge and said, "Nice shooting but don't ever do that again. The sailors in the engine room did not have time to respond to one engine order before you issued the next one. The entire engine room watch was exhausted by your constantly changing orders."

My pride of accomplishment was blown away by the Captain's rebuke. My ego fell as quickly as the yellow plane had gained altitude. I felt like the kid sitting on the edge of the bed 20 years before, mystified by being punished for something that had previously been OK.

I mulled over that four-hour watch for weeks. I tried to figure out what I could have done differently to receive only praise while avoiding any criticism. The best that I could conjure up was to go along with the norm. Issue only enough orders to keep the ship essentially on station and forego the accurate gunfire. This course of action would mean sacrificing the admiration of the Marines and the elation I felt when praised. However, the trade-off was a good one. Avoiding the death-like pain of the Captain's criticism was far preferable to any praise-evoked euphoria. This reasoning left me with the realization that the Vietnam war was as dishonorable as claimed by the war protestors. How could a war be righteous if physical exertion of sailors in an engine room was a reason to back off from killing the enemy? I began to think of the tens of thousands of American soldiers killed by Viet Cong and NVA. I thought of NVA bodies disappearing in a flash of light and a huge cloud of dust from our gunfire. I wondered if I had killed relatives of the peaceful fishermen who were all around us and seemed to want nothing more than to get on with their lives. I realized that my deliberate killing of NVA was an apostasy, an abandonment of my deeply held belief that all life is sacred. In defense of my sanity, I dispatched such thoughts as deeply into my interior being as I could. The shame at having killed human beings did not stay buried. For forty years I have thought of those North Vietnamese soldiers and the need for approval that inspired me to do the best job I could killing them. I cannot change these troubling facts. But I can change myself.

From where I stood
atop the sea cloud
the universe was a time-curved sphere
that had no center,
every direction
accelerating
back in time

disappearing beyond its outer-edged genesis
13.7 billion years ago.

Beyond the beach of distant stars
more distant suns withdraw
to an infrared before.

i stand amazed
that you and i,
beloved,
find ourselves
at this place
in this moment
conjoined.

Just before my 70th birthday I began taking classes in Tai Chi
Chih. The movement "Daughter on the Mountaintop is particularly
evocative. I imagine myself as a middle-aged Vietnamese woman,
perhaps a daughter of one of the soldiers I killed, standing atop
the Hải Vân crest, the tourmaline highest point in Vietnam. I
imagine the graceful sweeping rhythm of my arms and hands
bringing me to unity with the mountain peak and the life force
that surrounds me like an infinite orb. What could be more different
from the young Navy lieutenant that I was than a Vietnamese
woman paying homage to her homeland? It seems like an amend.
Imperfect as it is, for now it is the best I can do.

III. Inhabitation

He surprised me when he said, "Birmingham, Alabama" in
answer to my question. For one thing, Chuck had no detectable
Southern accent. For another, and more importantly, he did not fit
the image formed by my prejudice about Southerners. My experience
with folks from the South consisted of a week in Chattanooga,
Tennessee receiving an award for Berkeley High School as most
outstanding high school in the nation. I had been elected President of
the student body, so had the honor of making the trip. While in
the South, I was repeatedly asked about what it was like to attend
school with *nigras*. "Don't they smell?" sticks in my mind as a
question that was particularly disturbing. Knowing that Chuck
was from an even deeper Deep South state, I figured his attitudes
and ignorance could only be worse than what I had experienced in
Tennessee. But Chuck astounded me. He was soft spoken and
deplored the racial injustice perpetrated by "Bull" Conner, who
was the notoriously racist sheriff of Birmingham at the time.

Like me, Chuck was in the Navy ROTC because the Navy was paying his way through Stanford. We also had in common encouragement from families with a military heritage, though his was deeper, went back generations. Mine went back no further than my father. Through our college years, Chuck and I remained the sort of friends that are more than acquaintances, but less than intimate. I got to know him best when we went to Pensacola, Florida for flight training the summer between our sophomore and junior years. We competed for top marks (he was the winner) and compared notes often about the joys of flying airplanes. Denial obliterated any consciousness we may have had that one out of three Navy pilots died in combat. The Vietnam War seemed theoretical to both of us, and therefore irrelevant to our ambition to fly Navy jets. Our performance at flight school got us accepted into a pool of potential future aviators.

Our friendship began to dwindle as our paths diverged when we got back to Stanford in the fall. My vision was tested. It had deteriorated to 20/25 in both eyes, which meant I would have to wear glasses to fly. I was disqualified from further consideration to become a Navy pilot. Chuck did not suffer the same fate. After graduation in 1968 he returned to Pensacola to qualify as an F-4 Phantom pilot and was assigned to a carrier-based combat squadron. We lost contact with each other. I did not know Chuck was killed a year later during combat operations. At the time, I was enjoying a deferment from active duty to attend graduate school at UC Berkeley.

More than three decades passed before I learned of his death. Charles Taylor was featured in an article in an issue of the Stanford Magazine about veteran alumni killed in action. I was travelling to Washington D.C. on business when I read the article, so had an opportunity to visit the monolithic black Vietnam War Memorial wall to find his name. Since that visit, Chuck has inhabited my mind.

I think of Chuck often. When I do, I have a very clear image of him as he was fifty years ago, standing before me, in the direct and open manner that was so attractive about him. His stare seems imploring. I wonder if anyone remembers him. As far as I know he had no siblings; both of his parents must be dead by now. I have the thought that perhaps he is asking me to do something that no one else can do.

As I have been writing about these wartime experiences, his image has begun to fade slightly from my mind. Maybe it is a sign that I have done what he wanted. Perhaps he needed me to

tell his story, to tell that he was a kind and decent person and sorry
for killing. It is as if my writing about the war is an apology for
both of us.

my eyes close…

city rush subsides…

mind-framed dwarf camellia
wind-sigh envelops conscious
salmon pink star flowers
overspread yellow black bee buzz
drift on golden stamen
under long thunder jet rumble…

you enter
through thought dapples
on leaf shade…

dabs of pointillist meander
intensify sentience,
gather to center hush…

In distracted awareness
of your presence
my poem composes…

itself.

WESPAC Transit
Whit Schweizer

      I. Outbound

Nothing reminds me more of God's grace
than dolphins' joyful surfing on our bow wave
inviting with their arcing jumps
our grey behemoth to join the play
and I to leap from the bridge rail
into a sea of selfish freedom
there to be with flying fish,
fly faster than the ship can steam
in flight
from a predator.

There are places where sea salt dries black on our deck,
and our wake shines white on a moonless night.

      II. Inbound

On the midwatch my mind meandered
to thoughts of the NVA soldier
who ran in uniformed flight
along the Cửa Việt beach
just south of the DMZ,
escaping from what I did not know.
A mile or so away
I watched the soldier through binoculars
disappear in a geyser of sand, flesh, flame, and dust,
vaporized by a shore bombardment shell
shot from our 5"/54 caliber Mark 42 gun.

The soldier was blown from the beach to my brain,
where she advocates for peace.

The Wall
C. David Hay

Granite as black as the smoke of war,
A name to touch and cry,
An epitaph of sacrifice,
And still the question —Why?

Homage paid in special ways:
A rose — a note — a sigh,
Frustration wrought with anger
That fate chose these to die.

They never asked for glory,
Just a grave of homeland sod;
They gave their lives for Country,
Now they answer but to God.

Could tears but wash away the pain
And heal a Nation's scar,
That men may find a better way
Than futile acts of war.

Pray their death was not in vain—
A lesson to recall:
A future world without the need
Of names upon a Wall.

Only Soldiers Know...
Sandra Flores-Surprise

Only soldiers know
the sacred intimacy
of the fraternal banter between them.

On the frontlines,
in foreign foxholes,
in the mind-fuck jungles,
in jihadis' wadis,
in the belly of the Bradley,
in the Humvees;
at the devil's hour while pulling guard...
on patrol,
to feel some semblance of control.

Only soldiers know
the language of the disparaging,
barbed exchanges and the derisive dialogue.

the venting,
the cursing,
the insults,
the nicknames,
the ridicule,
the one-upping,
the crassness,
the callous jokes;
it's all prophylactic…

against all the action
they cannot process.

All with which they cannot come to terms
forges a brotherhood, a sisterhood, within The Suck.

It is the intrinsic phenomena,
that in and of itself,
creates the sacrament of
release,
decompression,
bonding;

a salve
for the passive-aggressive ways
the days
exact emotional, psychological
wounds.

Wounds,
like a thousand tiny paper cuts
imperceptible to the psyche.
wounds deeper than flesh,
that go unnoticed…even to themselves.

Though they must endeavor to, "Suck it up, buttercup!"

For tomorrow, they go out again
and witness fresh new hells.

Semper Canine
Rachael Ikins

1.
Paris, WW II, a soldier crawls into
an abandoned bakery to shelter from
bombs. As he shifts a cake box, something whimpers.
Unties the string, flips the lid. A tiny caterpillar
of a puppy, a note stuck under
 "Please take care of my dog, Chenille"
They came back home together.

2.
Desert soldier and his canine partner,
Dog a trained weapon worth thousands.
She sniffs for bombs and booby traps during
Missions. Bed-time she tugs her squeaky toy
then stretches out spooned with her human.

Once discharged he returns home without her.
Has trouble adjusting to civilian life, every car back-fire
or door slam he flinches, and once in the supermarket
he bellyflops under an end-cap, combat habits ingrained.
More powerful than reality.

He wonders how his partner is, guys from his unit send
pictures when they can. One day he learns she stepped
on a land mine. Lost her left front leg. Suddenly he needs
the scent and weight of her, her wet nose, her body curled
against his pounding chest. Much research and back and forthing,
the two former partners reunite in an airport,
folks watching applaud as dog and man
throw themselves into each other.
Later, his wife tells a reporter, "He is much calmer
now that she is here."

3.
He flinches every time a new dog is brought in, the kennels
overwhelming with stenches of fear and grief.
Some dogs wet themselves. Fawn at the humans.
He senses death. Days pass, concrete.
Run, barking, food. Strangers come and go.

He allows a tail wag to one worker only.
At night he runs and shivers as he dreams.
One sunny morning his worker helps a woman in a wheel chair
roll down the narrow aisles. He can sense her hope before he
sees her.

Her heart skips, filled with ghosts of fear. When the door slams,
she flinches, too. Her tires stop at his gate.

He can't help himself, he gives her his nose, pushed through the
chain link. She leans to touch so carefully. She knows a dog's
nose is sensitive. He raises amber eyes not daring to wish. When
his eyes meet her brown ones, he sees water streaking down her
face. She turns to his worker and says, " I knew a dog like this
when I was over there. A stray my buddies and I took in. Slept
in our tent. We fed him…"

Silence pauses the endless litany of dog-prayers. He pushes his
face closer into her hand. Skin that carries the faintest memory
of gun. She looks him in the eye and asks him, "Would you like
to come home with me?" He starts to wag. His whole back end
wags.

"I guess that is a 'yes'."
Leashed he walks next to her wheels. At the front desk, worker
says, "No adoption fee, Lieutenant. Not for vets. Congratulations."
Humans shake hands, then, his leash around her wrist he leads
her out into the sunshine.

CONTRIBUTORS

Ben Applebaum spent 8 years as an Active Duty US Army photographer, and is currently continuing his service in the Army Reserve.

Joan Applebaum is an artist who divides her time living in and painting her native Upstate New York and Coastal Delaware. She maintains an active teaching and exhibiting schedule for her business, Windy Hill Studio. 9www.windyhillstudioarts.com) She is the mother of a Marine who served 2009-2013 and a Soldier active duty 2011-2018, currently in Army Reserves.

Dario R. Beniquez, USA, USAF, Captain, Civil Engineering, was both in the Army and the Air Force. Currently retired from the USAF, he spends his time writing and running a Writers' Workshop at Gemini Ink Literary Arts Center, San Antonio, Texas.

Mark Blickley was a Sergeant in the US Air Force and a C-141 crew chief. He is a proud member of the Dramatist Guild and PEN American Center.

Mike Brady was an Air Force Officer and nine years after retirement he is something else altogether, more Buddha-ish and birdlike.

Bernie S. Conklin's uncles served in WW II in the Air Force and Army, as well as a brother who served in the Army and a nephew in the Navy. Born in Utica, Bernie owned and operated a small contracting company and raised 3 sons with his wife, Mary. He is a member of the Canastota Writers group.

William Conelly served active duty in the Regular Air Force at the Air Force Academy in Colorado Springs; afterwards he took both Bachelor's and Master's Degrees in English at the University of California, Santa Barbara, under the distinguished poet and former Army Translator Edgar Bowers.

Mike Dailey's mother served as an Army nurse in the jungles of New Guinea and the Philippines from 1942 until September 1945. She was in a MASH type unit (116th Station Hospital) often under fire.

Tony Daly retired as a Master Sergeant from Air Force Reserves in 2016 and is an Associate Editor with Military Experience and the Arts. Follow him on Twitter @aldaly18. Links to his published works are available at, https://aldaly13.wixsite.com/website.

Penny Lee Deere, SFC, US Army retired. Advocate, artist, writer, and song writer.

Dean C. Dickinson, Captain, U.S. Air Force with deployments to Guam, Trinidad, Spain, Italy, England, Saudi Arabia, and Turkey. Ramstein AB, Germany where his story takes place, (1961-1964.) He is the author of memoirs, *Corn and Me* and *The Moon and Me* and a member of the Canastota Writers Group.

Janet Fagal is a poet and retired teacher and the daughter of WW II Army Air Corpsman Felix M. Sangenito. Her poems appear in several anthologies. She is past president of the CNY Branch of the NLAPW (Pen Women.)

Laura Williams French is a poet, writer, and publisher whose father, Douglas W. Williams, served in the U.S. Navy aboard the U.S.S. Mississinewa from 1967-1968.

Dr. C. David Hay commemorates his poem to all who gave their lives in the service of their country in Viet Nam. God Bless them and the United States of America.

Patricia Hardigree is the mother-in-Law to Gipper Hugh Grimes, a Viet Nam veteran who passed away 1994. Her two eldest sons served in the Marines during peace time. Her youngest son Daryl was in the USAF and is very active in the Air National Guard.

Rachael Ikins' husband, father, uncles, and grandfather were all Army veterans of WW I and II. She is an award-winning poet and visual artist. She wore a POW bracelet during the Viet Nam war. Her soldier made it home. They corresponded and by amazing chance, years later on a PBS Memorial Day documentary, she saw her soldier, Capt. Robert Schumacher debark from his plane in Los Angeles when he returned.

Emmanuel Kane has published five books of poetry about war and love, including the highly acclaimed *Growing Flames, Fury & Lavende*r (P.R. A Press). He lives in Charlotte, North Carolina and speaks about the troubling impact of globalization on war veterans and local cultures

Mike Kanner retired from the US Army as a major after a career including assignments in Europe, Latin America and most of the United States. He is married to Paula, also retired Army as a major (who literally outranks him.)

Laurie Kolp is the wife of a former Marine. Her poetry books include *Upon the Blue Couch_*and chapbook *Hello, It's Your Mother*. An avid runner and nature lover, she lives in Texas with her family.

Frank Light served in Vietnam as a draftee with the U.S. Army. On retirement from government service he returned to the love of writing that led, years ago, to a master of fine arts in fiction. Twenty literary journals and anthologies have published adaptations from the draft memoir *Adjust to Dust: On the Backroads of Southern Afghanistan* from which this draws. A number of his poems, fiction, and other essays have also recently been published.

Maureen Teresa McCarthy, writer and poet, has been published in many journals. Currently at work on a novel of women in the Civil War, she is the daughter of Lt. Robert Q. McCarthy, United States Navy, who served during WW II.

Judith McGinn is a published writer and poet. Her late husband, Michael McGinn, USN Lieutenant did a tour of duty in Viet Nam. Her son Seamus McGinn is a Petty Officer 2nd Class in the US Navy and currently stationed near Tokyo.

Ronald Milburn is the younger brother of a Marine and sailor who fought in the Vietnam war.

Arthur Ramer's father served in the US Army in WW II as a translator. Arthur would best like to remembered as a poet who was proud of his dad's service.

Heidi Nightengale is an author and poet in the Finger Lakes region of CNY. She teaches for the State University of New York at Empire State College and is the co-owner and editor/ publisher of Clare Songbirds. She is the author of two children's books and two poetry chapbooks. Her uncle was killed in action during WW II.

Peggy Seely is a poet and author of *Teacups in the Mud* and *Wrestling with Ghosts* was a Navy wife in the early 1950s.

Tom Seely, QM2, served on the USS Maloy EDE 791 out of New London, CT during the Korean War years.

Kimberly Slaughter-Cunningham is a poet and author. She is niece to Sergeant Brian Wilson, E7, who served in the US Army for 20 years, 1970-1990.

Angela Sobery is the spouse of a Wounded Warrior veteran. Retired Navy 2015.

Sandra Flores-Surprise is the first and only woman in the history of her family to have served in any branch of the military. She served 6 years Active Duty in the United States Army. While stationed in Hawai'i she was subjected to Stop Loss on Oahu as a result of the events on September 11, 2001. Writing poetry is 'self -therapy' and a cathartic way to process, exam, cope with, and make sense of her life experiences. Sandra currently co-facilitates a Woman Veteran poetry group for writing as healing.

Fee Thomas is an internationally published poet and activist from North Minneapolis. Her debut book *Owning the Color Blue* is available through Clare Songbirds Publishing House. She is the granddaughter of a WW2 Veteran.

Katie Turner is a watercolor artist from Syracuse, NY married to Ralph Turner, Katie loves painting on slick surfaces. Her work is evocative, fresh and intuitive. www.KTArtStudio.com

Ralph Turner served 28 years with the US Army and the US Marine Corp. He completed a tour of duty in Operation Iraqi Freedom with the 138th Mobile Public Affairs Detachment. He is now retired and works for the NYS Dept. of Labor helping veterans find new jobs.

John Whitaker "Whit" Schweizer enlisted in the Navy Reserve in March 1963. He received his commission as a Navy Ensign in June 1968 and served on active duty as a Lieutenant from July 1970-October 1974. His active duty service included two tours in the Vietnam War theater.

Dwain Wilder builds musical instruments for a living, writes poetry, and edits a weekly newsletter for activists working on climate change who served in the Navy and was stationed at Naval Air Station Guantanamo Bay as an Aviation Electronics Technician, Petty Officer 2nd Class and served as navigation/radar/communications flight crew member on Search and Rescue missions. He later served as head of the Southern Coordinating Committee to End the War in Vietnam.

Catherine Zickgraf is a poet and author. Her husband served one tour of duty in Iraq and one year in Korea with the United States Army.

The publisher wishes to acknowledge the following publications where these works originally appeared.

"The Washing Machine," Dean C. Dickinson appeared first in his memoir *Corn and Me*

"Red Sun" Maureen T. McCarthy appeared first in *The Comstock Literary Review*

"The First Thanksgiving," appeared in Peggy Seeley's poetry collection, *Wrestling the Ghosts*, Foothills, 2016

"Lying the Truth," Mark Blickley first appeared as part of an audio book anthology *Yet We Persisted* and was a finalist for an Audie award for original book.

"Surprising Benediction," Janet Fagal, appeared first in The Pen Woman Magazine. "Atonal" was in the Pen Women Press anthology *Spirit, Peace, and Joy* and was Poem of the Week on NLAPW.org

"Medal Winner" William Conelly appeared previously in The Pedestal magazine and an anthology since.

"An Epitaph" William Conelly appeared in Skylight 47, Issue 10, Galway, Ireland, May 2018

"Labor Day" Dwain Wilder, first appeared in *Under the Only Moon,* Foothills Publishing

"Fourth Grade Autobiography 1969" Heidi Nightengale first appeared in *Tillable Soil,* Clare Songbirds Publishing House, 2017.

"Uniform" Fee Thomas appeared in *Owning the Color Blue*

The publisher wishes to thank the photographers whose photos appear in this book

Cover:
Seamus McGinn
Janet Fagal
Ralph Turner
Laura Williams French

Page 10:
Skeeze from Pixabay

Page 17:
Joan Applebaum

Page 34:
Skeeze from Pixabay

Page 58:
Frank Light

Page 76:
Keturah Moller from Pixabay

Page 86:
Skeeze from Pixabay

Page 110:
Ben Applebaum

Page 121:
Ben Applebaum

Page 136:
Skeeze from Pixabay

9 781947 653795